A Hundred Ways with Beef
The third volume of *Classic French Kitchen*

We eat more beef than any other meat, yet know least about it. We cook beef every day, yet are ignorant of all its different cuts. We hardly ever ask for it in forms other than steak, roast beef or stewing beef; but for butchers, cutting meat correctly is an art: beef appears in at least 29 ways, each of which has its own distinct appearance and taste, and it is intended for quite different dishes. Each one of these cuts has a particular name which we ought to know, so we do not have to follow recipes blindly – we should be able to select meat completely for ourselves. Then we will be able to prepare the same dish repeatedly, each time better than the last.

This third volume in the series 'Classic French Kitchen' is devoted entirely to beef and constitutes a valuable guide: each of the 100 recipes contained in it clearly states the cut of beef necessary for the execution of the dish. The hints given on these pages will enable you to make the right choice when buying your meat.

The various chapters of this book offer a vast range of gastronomic possibilities in the cooking of beef – in savoury grills, sumptuous roasts, pleasing sautés, succulent boiled dishes, exotic minced dishes and cold dishes that will surprise you by their excellence. But the place of honour here is reserved for the long-forgotten stew. With its long and slow simmering, it has the unique advantage of leaving you free to do other things while it cooks itself. The stew, which can easily be reheated without losing any of its flavour – indeed it often improves with reheating – is at one and the same time the traditional dish, the dish of family celebrations and homecomings, at the very heart of French provincial cooking.

From now on you will be able to combine the often modest elements that make sumptuous and delicious dishes. You no longer have to dream of delicious beef stews so tender that you need only a spoon to eat them. From now on, you can cook them.

Table of Contents

Each dish is followed by its total preparation and cooking time. (See note 1 on facing page.)

The star (★) system used throughout the book, indicating the degree of simplicity or difficulty of each recipe, is as follows:

★ *Very easy*   ★★ *Easy*   ★★★ *Difficult*

Classic French Kitchen: Number 3

A Hundred Ways with Beef

112 step-by-step recipes

 Ferndale Editions, London

French and English cuts of beef

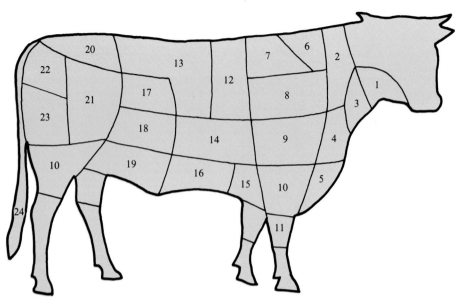

1. *Joue*
2. *Talon de collier*
3. *Collier*
4. *Griffe*
5. *Poitrine*
6. *Basses côtes*
7. *Entrecôte*
8. *Paleron*
9. *Jumeau et macreuse*
10. *Gîte-gîte*
11. *Crosse*
12. *Côtes couvertes*
13. *Faux-filet*
14. *Plat de côtes*
15. *Milieu de poitrine*
16. *Tendron*
17. *Filet*
18. *Bavette*
19. *Flanchet*
20. *Rumsteck*
21. *Tranche*
22. *Culotte*
23. *Gîte à la noix*
24. *Queue*

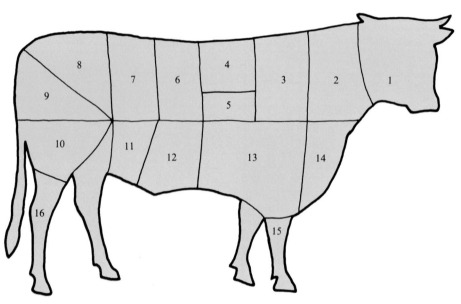

1. *Head and cheek*
2. *Neck*
3. *Chuck*
4. *Middle rib*
5. *Top rib*
6. *Prime fore rib*
7. *Sirloin*
8. *Rump*
9. *Aitchbone*
10. *Topside and silverside*
11. *Thick flank*
12. *Thin flank*
13. *Brisket*
14. *Clod*
15. *Shin*
16. *Leg*

Notes: Getting the Best out of this Book

1. The preparation times given in the Table of Contents and with each recipe are minimum times: they will vary according to the cook's ability and the equipment available. Certain of the recipes require periods for marinading or chilling. These have not been taken into account in the times given in the table, but are indicated at the head of each recipe.

2. It is always best to use red or white wine vinegar in the recipes where vinegar is required; the results will not be the same if you use malt vinegar. In the same way, freshly ground black pepper should always be used in preference to ready-ground pepper.

3. Oven temperatures. The following are Gas, Fahrenheit and Centigrade equivalents:

Gas	¼	½	1	2	3	4	5	6	7	8	9
°F	225	250	275	300	325	350	375	400	425	450	475
°C	110	120	140	160	170	180	190	200	220	230	250

4. It is important when using these recipes to follow the exact proportions. A set of kitchen scales, measuring jug, glass and spoons are essential. Follow either metric *or* avoirdupois measurements in each recipe.

5. To help you choose the right wine for your meal, see page 80.

Filet aux Cèpes à la Braise

Serves 4. Preparation: 3 min Cooking: 10 min

Grilled Fillet with Mushrooms

★

○ **4 fillet steaks, 200g (7 oz) each**
○ **4 large mushrooms**
○ **15ml (1 tbls) oil**
○ **salt**

1. Remove the stalks from the mushrooms (save them and use them for stuffing, sauces or omelettes). Wipe the mushrooms with a damp cloth. Brush the mushrooms and steaks with oil.
2. Cook under a grill or on a barbecue. Start cooking the mushrooms first: place them hollow side up on the grill and cook for 10 minutes. Cook the steaks for 4 minutes (rare) to 7 minutes (well done). Add salt after 5 minutes.
3. When the meat and mushrooms are cooked, place the steaks on a dish and decorate each with a mushroom. Serve at once.

These steaks can be served with a dash of olive oil or a knob of butter, seasoned with a little garlic, anchovy paste and herbs.

Tournedos Maître d'Hôtel

Serves 4. Preparation: 10 min Cooking: 8 min

Grilled Tournedos with Parsley Butter Sauce

★

○ **4 tournedos, 150g (5 oz) each**
○ **100g (4 oz) butter**
○ **30ml (2 tbls) roughly chopped parsley or mixed herbs**
○ **15ml (1 tbls) lemon juice**
○ **15ml (1 tbls) strong French mustard**
○ **salt and pepper**

1. Heat the grill or barbecue.
2. Cut the butter into small cubes and place in a small saucepan over a low heat. Whip with a whisk or fork till it acquires a creamy consistency. Remove from the heat and add the lemon juice and mustard, beating constantly. Add salt, pepper and parsley. Mix again and pour into a sauceboat.
3. Place the tournedos on the hot grill. Cook for 5 minutes (rare) to 8 minutes (well done). Place them on a serving dish. Salt them and serve at once. Each person tops his or her tournedos with a spoonful of parsley butter sauce which will melt on contact.

Entrecôte à la Florentine

Serves 2. Preparation and cooking: 15 min

Rib Steak Florentine Style

★

○ **1 rib steak**
○ **olive oil**
○ **salt and pepper**

1. Place the meat on a large dish. Sprinkle with oil, season with plenty of freshly ground pepper and leave to marinate for 10 minutes.
2. Heat the grill (for best results cook over a wood fire). Add the meat and cook for 3-4 minutes on each side. Salt just before removing from the heat and serve immediately, on a hot dish.

Araignée Mignonnette

Serves 2. Preparation: 5 min Cooking: 3-4 min

Steak Mignonnette

★

○ **2 steaks**
○ **10ml (2 tsp) coarsely ground pepper**
○ **5ml (1 tsp) olive oil**
○ **salt**

1. Preheat the grill. Brush the steaks with oil. Press the pepper well into the meat, making sure it sticks.
2. When the grill is very hot, cook the steak for 1½ to 2 minutes each side, depending on whether you like your meat rare or well done.
3. When the steaks are cooked, season and serve immediately.

The steaks may be basted with a little olive oil whilst cooking. Serve with grilled tomatoes and pommes frites. Alternatively serve with a knob of butter and garnish with cress.

Hampe au Persil

Serves 4. Preparation: 10 min Cooking: 2-4 min

Flank with Parsley Sauce

★

○ **2 pieces of flank, 350g (12 oz) each**
○ **60ml (4 tbls) roughly chopped parsley**
○ **60ml (4 tbls) double cream**
○ **10ml (2 tsp) French mustard**
○ **5ml (1 tsp) crushed peppercorns**
○ **nutmeg**
○ **salt**

1. Heat the grill. Place the mustard in a small saucepan. Add the cream, salt, nutmeg to taste, pepper and parsley. Mix well.
2. When the grill is very hot, place the meat on it and cook for 1 minute (rare) to 2 minutes (well done). (This cut of meat is very flat and therefore cooks very quickly, hence the necessity for a very hot grill.)
3. While the meat is cooking, place the saucepan on a very low heat and heat the sauce, without allowing it to boil.
4. When the meat is cooked, cut each steak into two. Arrange them on a serving dish and cover with parsley sauce. Serve immediately.

This dish can be served with jacket potatoes: they are delicious with the parsley sauce.

Bavette à la Vinaigrette Verte

Serves 4. Preparation: 15 min Cooking: 4-7 min

Top of Sirloin with Green Vinaigrette

★

○ **4 top of sirloin steaks, 150 to 200g (5-7 oz) each**
○ **60ml (4 tbls) olive oil**
○ **15ml (1 tbls) sherry vinegar (if available, otherwise substitute white wine vinegar)**
○ **1 clove garlic**
○ **1 small onion**
○ **30ml (2 tbls) chopped parsley**
○ **15ml (1 tbls) chopped herbs: chervil or chives**
○ **cayenne pepper**
○ **salt and freshly ground pepper**

1. Peel the garlic and onion. Chop the onion as finely as possible. Put the garlic through a press and collect the juice in a bowl. Add the oil and vinegar, salt, pepper and cayenne to taste. Whip until the mixture is creamy, then add the parsley, chervil or chives and onion. Mix again. Allow the sauce to stand for 1 hour before serving.
2. Heat a grill or barbecue. Grill the steaks for 4 minutes (rare) to 7 minutes (well done), according to their thickness. Arrange them on individual plates or on one dish and serve immediately. Serve the parsley sauce separately.

A small spoonful of anchovy paste may be added to the sauce and a small fresh chopped red pepper may be substituted for the cayenne.

Pavés au Jus d'Ail

Serves 4. Preparation: 10 min Cooking: 6-8 min

Rump Steak with Garlic

★

○ **4 rump steaks, 180g (6 oz) each**
○ **6 cloves garlic**
○ **6 drops Tabasco sauce**
○ **45ml (3 tbls) olive oil**
○ **salt and pepper**

1. Ask your butcher to cut 4 steaks from one slice of meat. You will get thick pieces with right angles – 'slabs'.
2. Pour the oil into a small bowl. Add plenty of pepper and the Tabasco sauce. Peel the garlic cloves and put them through a garlic press. Add to the oil and beat with a fork until creamy.
3. Heat a grill or a barbecue. Brush the steaks with the oil mixture and place them on the grill. Cook the steaks for 3 minutes (rare) to 4 minutes (well done) on each side.
4. When the steaks are cooked, add salt, arrange them on individual plates and serve immediately.

Châteaubriands Béarnaise

Serves 4. Preparation and cooking: 40 min

Porterhouse Steaks with Béarnaise Sauce

★★★

○ **4 porterhouse steaks, 200g (7 oz) each**
○ **200g (7 oz) butter**
○ **3 egg yolks**
○ **100ml (3½ fl oz) white wine**
○ **100ml (3½ fl oz) tarragon vinegar**
○ **15ml (1 tbls) shallots, chopped very fine**
○ **5ml (1 tsp) freshly ground pepper**
○ **1 sprig tarragon**
○ **salt**

1. Cut the butter into small cubes and place it in a small saucepan. Wash and chop the tarragon. Put aside.
2. Place the shallots, vinegar, wine and pepper into another saucepan and place over a low heat. Allow this mixture to boil slowly until 15ml (1 tbls) liquid remains (this takes about 10 minutes), then remove from the heat and allow to cool for 2 minutes.
3. While this mixture is cooling, place the saucepan containing the butter on the heat until it is completely melted.
4. Heat the grill. Place the egg yolks into the saucepan containing the shallot mixture. Place on an asbestos mat on a very low heat and beat continuously with a whisk for 5-6 minutes, until the mixture is creamy. If the heat is too high in spite of the asbestos mat, remove the saucepan from the heat at intervals. It is essential that the heat is very gentle for this sauce.
5. When the mixture is creamy, add salt to taste, then the butter in small pieces, beating constantly. When the butter has been absorbed, the sauce is ready. Pass the sauce through a sieve into a sauceboat, pressing with the back of a spoon to extract all the shallot juices. Add the tarragon.
6. Grill the steaks for 4 minutes (rare) to 7 minutes (well done). Arrange them on a serving dish and serve immediately. Serve the sauce separately.

Faux-Filet à l'Infusion d'Herbes

Serves 2. Preparation: 10 min
Cooking: 4-6 min Marinade: 20 min

Sirloin Steak with Herbs

★

○ **2 slices sirloin steak, 200g (7 oz) each**
○ **10ml (2 tsp) thyme**
○ **10ml (2 tsp) rosemary**
○ **2 bay leaves, crumbled**
○ **2 cloves**
○ **2 chili peppers, crumbled**
○ **1 star anise, sliced**
○ **8ml (1 heaped tsp) salt**
○ **5ml (1 tsp) freshly ground pepper**

1. Place thyme, rosemary, bay leaves, cloves, star anise, chili peppers, salt and pepper in a small saucepan. Add 150ml (5 fl oz) water and place the saucepan over a medium heat. Boil for 1 minute, remove from the heat and allow to cool.
2. When the mixture is cold, strain through a fine strainer into a bowl and place the steaks on top. Allow them to marinate for 20 minutes, turning once. Meanwhile, heat the grill to a high temperature.
3. When the grill is very hot, drain the steaks without wiping them dry, and seal them for 1 minute each side, then cook for a further 3 minutes (rare) to 5 minutes (well done).
4. When the steaks are cooked, arrange them on individual plates and serve immediately.

Serve with a selection of vegetables in season: buttered green beans, sautéed courgettes, baked tomatoes, grilled mushrooms.

Entrecôte à l'Échalote

Rib Steak with Shallots

★ ★

○ **1 rib steak, 500g (18 oz)**
○ **8 shallots**
○ **100ml (3½ fl oz) wine vinegar**
○ **5ml (1 tsp) freshly ground pepper**
○ **5ml (1 tsp) French mustard**
○ **5ml (1 tsp) chopped tarragon**
○ **80g (3¼ oz) butter**
○ **salt**

1. Peel and finely chop the shallots. Place them in a small saucepan with the pepper, 2.5ml (½ tsp) salt, tarragon and vinegar.
2. Heat the grill. When it is very hot, place the steak on it and grill for 5 minutes (rare) to 8 minutes (well done).
3. Meanwhile, place the saucepan over a high flame and reduce the vinegar mixture for 3 minutes until only 7-8ml (½ tbls) remains. Remove from the heat and add the mustard and the butter cut into small pieces, beating constantly with a fork. The mixture should be creamy.
4. When the steak is cooked, place it on a board and cut it crosswise into 8 thin slices. Arrange on a serving dish. Coat the meat with the shallot butter and serve immediately.

Côte de Boeuf au Beurre Bercy

Rib of Beef with Bercy Butter

★ ★

○ **1 rib of beef, about 1.2kg (2½ lb)**
○ **200g (7 oz) beef marrow**
○ **150ml (5 fl oz) dry white wine**
○ **4 grey shallots**
○ **120g (4½ oz) soft butter**
○ **15ml (1 tbls) chopped parsley**
○ **15ml (1 tbls) lemon juice**
○ **salt and pepper**

1. Ask the butcher for one of the first cuts off the side, so that you get a piece that is very wide and not too thick in relation to its weight. Trim the fat off but leave the knuckle bone attached.
2. Heat the grill or prepare a barbecue. Peel the shallots and chop as finely as possible. Cut the beef marrow into small cubes, 1cm (½ inch) square.
3. When the grill is hot, seal the beef for 2 minutes on each side, then, according to the thickness of the meat, cook for 15 to 20 minutes. Once sealed, either place the meat further away from the heat or lower the heat to avoid burning. When it is cooked, the meat is puffed up but firm to the touch.
4. While the meat is cooking, prepare the Bercy butter. Heat some salted water in a saucepan. When it starts to bubble, poach the marrow for 5 minutes. Do not let it boil. Remove from the heat with a skimmer and drain in a strainer. Place the shallots in a saucepan with the wine and reduce to half their quantity over a low heat, allow to cool to lukewarm, then add the butter while beating with a fork. Add the parsley, salt, pepper and lemon juice. Mix well and add the marrow. Mix again and pour the sauce into a sauceboat.
5. When the meat is cooked, serve in one piece or cut the meat in thin slices crosswise first but re-form as one whole piece on the dish. Serve the sauce separately.

To make a *marchand de vin* sauce, substitute a full-bodied red wine for the white, and increase the quantity of butter by 100g (4 oz). Omit the marrow.

Fillet Grilled with Rosemary (p13) ▶

Côte Marinée aux Oignons Dorés

Serves 4. Preparation and cooking: 50 min
Marinade: 4-6 hr
★

Marinated Rib of Beef with Golden Onions

○ **1kg (2¼ lb) rib of beef**
○ **30ml (2 tbls) vinegar**
○ **60ml (4 tbls) olive oil**
○ **2 bay leaves, crumbled**
○ **5ml (1 tsp) thyme**
○ **5ml (1 tsp) freshly ground pepper**
○ **6 large onions**
○ **15ml (1 tbls) strong French mustard**
○ **100g (4 oz) double cream**
○ **2.5ml (½ tsp) curry powder**
○ **50g (2 oz) butter**
○ **salt**

1. 4-6 hours in advance, prepare the marinade. Place the vinegar, oil, thyme, bay leaf and pepper in a bowl. Beat with a fork until the mixture is creamy.
2. Place the meat in a dish and pour over half the marinade. Turn the meat over and coat the other side with the remaining marinade. Put the dish in the refrigerator for 4-6 hours, turning it over once or twice during this time.
3. Take the meat out of the refrigerator 1 hour before cooking. 45 minutes before serving, peel the onions and mince them. Put them into a frying pan and allow them to 'sweat', turning them continuously for 5 minutes over a low heat. Then add the butter and cook over a low heat for 15 minutes. Add the cream and the curry powder and allow to simmer for 5 minutes.
4. Meanwhile, prepare the coals of a barbecue or heat the grill. Wipe the beef, then grill it for 12 minutes (rare) to 15 minutes (well done) on each side. Turn it over halfway through cooking. Do not place the meat too close to the heat.
5. When the meat is cooked, arrange on a serving dish. Pour the contents of the frying pan into a sauceboat and serve immediately.

Serve this dish with salads or vegetables in season: buttered green beans, baked tomatoes, grilled mushrooms.

Brochettes Sauce Piquante

Serves 4. Preparation: 10 min Cooking: 15 min

Kebabs with Piquant Sauce

★

○ **500g (18 oz) rump steak or fillet**
○ **200g (7 oz) smoked bacon**
○ **3 medium-sized onions**
○ **100ml (3½ fl oz) wine vinegar**
○ **30ml (2 tbls) tomato purée**
○ **2.5ml (½ tsp) freshly ground pepper**
○ **2.5ml (½ tsp) cayenne pepper**
○ **60g (2¼ oz) butter**
○ **2.5ml (½ tsp) sugar**
○ **5ml (1 tsp) salt**

1. Cut the bacon into strips ½cm (¼ inch) wide. Cut the meat into cubes 3cm (1¼ inches) square. Peel the onions and chop them as finely as possible.
2. Put the onions into a small saucepan with the vinegar, salt, sugar and pepper. Place the saucepan on a low heat and allow to simmer until the vinegar is reduced by half (about 5 minutes).
3. Add the tomato purée, 30ml (2 tbls) water and the cayenne pepper and allow to simmer for 5 minutes over a low heat.
4. Meanwhile, heat the grill or prepare a barbecue. Thread the cubes of meat and the strips of bacon onto skewers.
5. When the grill is hot, cook the kebabs for 5-6 minutes, turning often.
6. When the sauce is ready, add the butter, cut in small pieces. Whip the mixture until it is creamy. Pour the sauce into a sauceboat.
7. When the kebabs are cooked, arrange them on a serving dish and serve immediately with the sauce separately.

Serve with creole rice or with a green salad, grilled peppers or chips. Chopped herbs may be added to the sauce.

Filet à la Robespierre
Fillet Grilled with Rosemary

Serves 4. Preparation and cooking: 10 min

★

- ○ **2 slices of fillet, 180g (6 oz) each**
- ○ **olive oil**
- ○ **salt and freshly ground pepper**
- ○ **rosemary**

1. Sprinkle the meat generously with oil and pepper. Cook on a heated grill for 2-3 minutes each side, turning once, and adding the salt at the end of cooking.
2. Arrange sprigs of fresh rosemary on a warmed serving dish and sprinkle with oil. When the meat is cooked, place on the dish and turn 2 or 3 times in the rosemary so that the herb flavours the meat.
3. Finally, cut the meat into thin slices, having removed the rosemary. Pour over the cooking juices and serve immediately.

Rosbif aux Fruits
Roast Beef with Fruit

Serves 4. Preparation and cooking: 50 min

★★

- ○ **1 piece of sirloin, 800g (1¾ lb)**
- ○ **15ml (1 tbls) oil**
- ○ **salt and pepper**
- ○ **juice of 1 lemon**
- ○ **2 apples**
- ○ **2 bananas**
- ○ **3 oranges**
- ○ **50g (2 oz) butter**

1. Bind the meat with kitchen thread so it will keep its shape during cooking. Place in a dish, baste with oil, add salt and pepper and put aside. Preheat the oven to 230°C (450°F; gas mark 8).
2. Prepare the fruit. Pour the lemon juice into a bowl. Slice and core the apples and place in the lemon juice to prevent discolouring. Peel the bananas, cut into rounds and add to the apples. Peel the oranges, divide into segments, remove the pith and put aside.
3. Butter an ovenproof dish large enough to hold all the fruit in one layer 1cm (½ inch) thick. Remove the fruit from the lemon juice and mix with the orange segments. Melt the remaining butter and pour evenly over the fruit. Spread the fruit over the base of the ovenproof dish. Arrange the meat on top of the fruit and place the dish in the oven for 35 minutes. Remove the meat from the oven, allow to rest for 5 minutes, then slice and arrange on a serving dish. Surround the meat with the fruit.

Pièce de Boeuf à l'Oignon
Pot Roast with Onions

Serves 4. Preparation: 30 min Cooking: 2 hr 30 min

★

- ○ **800g (1¾ lb) rolled brisket or silverside**
- ○ **1kg (2¼ lb) red onions**
- ○ **200g (7 oz) butter**
- ○ **1 beef stock cube**
- ○ **salt and pepper**

1. Place the meat in a large saucepan, with the butter which has been cut into small pieces. Chop the onion finely, and cover the meat with them. Place over a low heat and turn the meat frequently.
2. Dissolve the stock cube in hot water. When the butter and the juice from the onions has nearly evaporated, add a little of the stock, and season. Leave to cook for about 2 hours 30 minutes. Remove the meat and pass the onions through a sieve or blender.
3. Slice the meat. Arrange on a serving dish and pour the hot purée over. Serve at once.

Rosbif à l'Anglaise
Roast Beef English Style

Serves 4. Preparation and cooking: 40 min

★

○ **800g (1¾ lb) fillet (for roasting)**
○ **100g (4 oz) butter**
○ **salt and pepper**

1. Trim the fat from the meat and bind with kitchen thread so that it will hold its shape.
2. Melt the butter in a stewpan and when it browns add the meat. Cook over a high flame for exactly 30 minutes: the meat should brown evenly all over. Turn the meat with a spatula to avoid piercing it. If you wish, baste with a little brandy and add a little water if necessary.
3. 5 minutes before the meat is cooked, salt and pepper it lightly, then place on a plate, cover with a second plate, and place a weight on the top. Collect the blood extracted from the meat, add to the cooking juices and heat, adding a little water if necessary, then pour into a heated sauceboat.
4. Slice the beef thinly (it should be lukewarm and red at the centre), place on a serving dish and serve the hot gravy separately. If you wish, surround with green vegetables.

The 'classic' English way to prepare roast beef allows a maximum of 40 minutes cooking time per kilo (2¼ lb) meat. If you don't like very rare meat, it can be cooked for a longer period.

Rosbif au Sel
Roast Beef Cooked in Salt

Serves 4. Preparation: 10 min Cooking: 1 hr 30 min

★

○ **800g (1¾ lb) rib of beef**
○ **6kg (13½ lb) coarse salt**

1. Preheat the oven to 300°C (550°F; gas mark 12). Trim the fat from the meat. Fill an oval flameproof dish with salt. Place the meat in the centre. Cover the meat completely with the remaining salt and place in the oven. During cooking, the salt will first melt and then form a crust.
2. Cook for 1 hour 30 minutes. Then remove the dish from the oven, break the crust with a knife so that it comes away from the edges of the dish and remove the salt from the meat with a pounder. Cut the meat into thick slices and serve.

This method is a variation of clay-baked roast. You may keep the salt and use for other dishes, but remember that it retains the flavour of the meat.

Meat of good quality is recognizable by its bright red colour and its layer of covering fat which should be thick and white or pale yellow. The older the animal, the darker the meat. Good meat looks smooth and has a slight sheen. It is criss-crossed by little veins of fat (when it is said to be 'marbled'). It should be slightly elastic and firm to the touch. Meat that is too lean or flabby, too light or too dark is not good-quality meat.

Roast Beef with Fruit (p13) ▶

Faux-Filet Poivre et Sel

Serves 6. Preparation: 5 min Cooking: 30 min

Sirloin Steak with Salt and Pepper

★

○ **1 slice sirloin steak, 1.3kg (2¾ lb)**
○ **30ml (2 tbls) green peppercorns**
○ **15ml (1 tbls) thyme**
○ **15ml (1 tbls) olive oil**
○ **500g (18 oz) coarse sea salt**

1. Ask the butcher to tie up the meat. Preheat the oven to 250°C (475°F; gas mark 9). Crush the peppercorns in a mortar with a pestle.
2. Oil the meat and press the pepper onto both sides with the palm of your hand to make it stick.
3. Mix the salt and thyme. Pour this into an ovenproof pan just large enough to hold the meat and put it in the oven. You will notice the delicious smell of thyme almost immediately.
4. Wait for 10 minutes, until the salt is fairly hot, then place the meat on it and cook for 15 minutes, first on one side and then the other – having turned it over without piercing it – and then for another 15 minutes to obtain well-done meat. If you like it rare, cook for 3 minutes less each side.
5. When the meat is cooked, turn off the oven and remove the meat. Place the meat on a rack over the dripping in the pan, and put it back in the oven. Allow the meat to rest for 10-15 minutes in the turned-off oven, turning it once during this time.
6. Serve thinly sliced, hot or cold.

This roast can be accompanied by sautéed mushrooms or tomatoes stuffed with garlic and breadcrumbs, and with various butter mixtures: garlic butter, mustard butter, anchovy butter, etc.

Rôti Enrobé de Moutarde

Serves 6. Preparation: 5 min Cooking: 35 min

Roast Beef with Mustard Sauce

★

○ **1 piece of rump for roasting, 1.2kg (2½ lb), bound**
○ **45ml (3 tbls) strong French mustard**
○ **15ml (1 tbls) freeze-dried green peppercorns**
○ **200g (7 oz) double cream**
○ **1 sprig tarragon**
○ **60ml (4 tbls) port**
○ **15ml (1 tbls) oil**
○ **salt**

1. Preheat the oven to 250°C (475°F; gas mark 9). Crush the peppercorns in a mortar with a pestle. Add the mustard and 15ml (1 tbls) cream. Mix well.
2. Oil an ovenproof dish which is just big enough to hold the roast. Spread the pepper mixture all over the roast, place it in the dish and place in the oven. Cook for 30 minutes (rare) to 35 minutes (well done). After 10 minutes of cooking, add half the port to the base of the dish; add the remainder 15 minutes later.
3. When the roast is cooked, turn the oven off and leave the meat to rest in the oven for 10 minutes, then place on a serving dish. Remove the string and place the dish in the lukewarm oven to keep it warm while the sauce is being prepared.
4. Pour the rest of the cream into the ovenproof dish and place the dish over a gentle heat. Mix well with a spatula, scraping up the crusty bits on the bottom, and allow the sauce to reduce by one-third. Meanwhile, wash the tarragon, dry it and roughly chop the leaves.
5. When the sauce is ready add salt to taste and the tarragon, pour it into a sauceboat and serve with the roast.

Rosbif au Yorkshire Pudding

Serves 6. Preparation and cooking: 2 hr

Roast Beef with Yorkshire Pudding

★★

- ○ **1 side of beef, 2kg (4½ lb), bound**
- ○ **220g (8 oz) flour**
- ○ **400ml (14 fl oz) milk**
- ○ **3 eggs**
- ○ **5ml (1 tsp) salt**

1. Preheat the oven to 280°C (525°F; gas mark 11). Prepare the Yorkshire pudding: place the flour in a bowl and break the eggs into the centre. Add salt and milk, whisking with a spatula. Leave to stand until ready to cook.
2. When the oven is hot, place the meat, fat side up, on a rack placed over a roasting pan. Allow to cook for 15 minutes at 280°C, then lower the heat to 200°C (400°F; gas mark 6) and allow another 40 minutes to 1 hour for cooking, according to whether the meat is preferred rare or well done.
3. When the meat is cooked, turn off the oven and leave the meat to rest inside for 5 minutes, then take it out, wrap it in several layers of aluminium foil and leave it in the drawer at the bottom of the oven or in some other warm place.
4. Relight the oven to 230°C (450°F; gas mark 8). Take 45ml (3 tbls) dripping and pour into a gratin dish large enough to contain the batter. Spread the fat evenly over the base and round the edges of the dish. Pour the batter in and place the dish in the oven for 15 minutes, then lower the heat to 220°C (400°F; gas mark 6) and continue cooking for another 15 minutes.
5. When the pudding is golden and well risen, place the meat on a board, cut the string, slice thickly and serve with the pudding.

This typically English roast can be served with a horseradish sauce prepared with 150g (5 fl oz) double cream, whipped and mixed with salt, pepper, a pinch of sugar, 5ml (1 tsp) mustard and 45ml (3 tbls) grated horseradish, fresh or dried.

Rôti en Cocotte

Serves 4. Preparation: 15 min Cooking: 45 min

Casseroled Roast Beef

★

- ○ **1 piece of rump for roasting, 2kg (4½ lb), bound**
- ○ **3 medium-sized carrots**
- ○ **2 medium-sized onions**
- ○ **1 celery heart**
- ○ **1 sprig thyme**
- ○ **1 bay leaf**
- ○ **30ml (2 tbls) oil**
- ○ **50g (2 oz) butter**
- ○ **salt and pepper**

1. Preheat the oven to 250°C (475°F; gas mark 9). Peel the carrots and slice them so thinly that they are transparent, or grate them. Peel the onions and mince them as finely as possible. Wash the celery heart and, without pulling off the outside stalks, cut into very thin slices. Mix all the vegetables together.
2. Heat the oil in an oval pot just large enough to hold the roast. Quickly brown the meat all over on a high heat for 5 minutes, taking care not to pierce the meat while it is being turned.
3. When the meat is lightly browned, remove it from the pot and place on a plate. Season the meat. Discard the oil in which it was cooked and replace this with the butter. Add the vegetables to the pot. Cook over a high flame for 2 minutes, add salt, pepper, the thyme and the bay leaf. Place the meat over the bed of vegetables. Cover the pot and place in the oven. Allow to cook for 25 minutes (rare) to 35 minutes (well done).
4. When the roast is cooked, cut the string, arrange the meat on a serving dish and surround it with the still slightly crisp vegetables.

Filet aux Trois Légumes Glacés

Serves 6. Preparation: 20 min Cooking: 40 min

Fillet with Three Glazed Vegetables

★★

- ○ 1kg (2¼ lb) fillet steak, barded and bound
- ○ 24 small new onions
- ○ 24 small new carrots
- ○ 24 small new turnips
- ○ 1 large onion
- ○ 1 large carrot
- ○ 15ml (1 tbls) granulated sugar
- ○ 15ml (1 tbls) oil
- ○ 150g (5 oz) butter
- ○ 100ml (3½ fl oz) Madeira
- ○ salt and pepper

1. Peel the large carrot and cut into thin rounds. Oil an ovenproof dish and cover it with the carrot rounds. Peel the large onion, mince it very finely and add to the dish. Place the roast on top.
2. Preheat the oven to 230°C (450°F; gas mark 8). Peel the new vegetables and cut them into rounds or ovals of the same size, to ensure that they cook evenly.
3. Place the roast in the oven. Take 3 saucepans, just large enough to hold each sort of new vegetable in one layer. Place each vegetable with 40g (1¾ oz) butter in a separate pan and sauté over a medium heat until the vegetables are golden brown, about 5 minutes, turning with a spatula.
4. When the vegetables are golden, sprinkle each with 5ml (1 tsp) sugar and 2.5ml (½ tsp) salt and cover with water. Allow to cook for 20-25 minutes, according to their size, until there is no water left in the pan and the vegetables are tender and glazed. Keep them hot until the meat is done.
5. After 30 minutes of cooking the roast is rare. After 35 minutes it is medium. When it is cooked as desired, turn the oven off and leave the roast to rest in the closed oven for at least 10 minutes.
6. Arrange the roast on a serving dish, untie the string and surround the meat with the glazed vegetables. Keep warm in the oven while you prepare the gravy: add 100ml (3½ fl oz) water and the Madeira to the ovenproof dish and place the dish over a high heat, scraping the bottom to make a gravy. Turn off the heat and add the remaining 30g (1¼ oz) butter. Mix, add salt and pepper to taste, and pour into a sauceboat through a fine strainer. Serve at once.

Filet en Croûte

Serves 4. Preparation and cooking: 1 hr 40 min

Fillet Steak in Puff Pastry

★★

- ○ 400g (14 oz) puff pastry, frozen or home-made
- ○ 50g (2 oz) dried mushrooms
- ○ 120g (4½ oz) butter
- ○ salt and pepper
- ○ 300ml (10 fl oz) beef stock
- ○ 700g (1½ lb) fillet in 1 piece
- ○ brandy
- ○ French mustard
- ○ 100g (4 oz) raw ham
- ○ 1 egg yolk

1. Thaw the pastry, if frozen. Meanwhile, soak the dried mushrooms in tepid water for 30 minutes. Wash thoroughly, drain and sauté in 40g (1¾ oz) melted butter. When lightly browned, add salt and pepper and pour in a ladleful of hot beef stock. Cook for 20 minutes, adding more stock if necessary. Then remove from the heat. Pour into a liquidizer and blend to a purée.
2. Preheat the oven to 200°C (400°F; gas mark 6). Melt the remaining butter in a sauté pan. When almost black, add the fillet and brown lightly on all sides, trying not to pierce the meat. Sprinkle brandy over the meat, allow to evaporate, then add salt and pepper to taste. Remove from the heat and put aside. Roll out the pastry in one piece, not too thin but large enough to cover the fillet.
3. Remove the meat from the pan and place on a dish. Spread completely with a thin layer of mustard, then wrap in slices of raw ham. Spread some of the mushroom purée on the pastry, place the meat on top and cover with the remaining mushroom purée. Fold the pastry over the meat to form a roll and flatten slightly. Decorate this with shapes made from any remaining pastry. Glaze with beaten egg yolk. Lift the roll carefully and place on a moistened baking sheet.
4. Place in the oven and cook for 40 minutes. When cooked, remove from the oven, place on a hot serving dish and serve immediately. Carve in front of your guests.

Filet à la Broche aux Trois Poivres

Fillet Steak with Three Peppers on a Spit

Serves 6. Preparation: 10 min
Cooking: 30 min
★

- ○ **1.2kg (2½ lb) beef fillet, bound**
- ○ **10ml (2 tsp) black peppercorns**
- ○ **10ml (2 tsp) white peppercorns**
- ○ **10ml (2 tsp) green peppercorns**
- ○ **15ml (1 tbls) oil**
- ○ **50ml (1¾ fl oz) armagnac**
- ○ **2 shallots**
- ○ **15ml (1 tbls) French mustard**
- ○ **150g (5 oz) double cream**
- ○ **50g (2 oz) butter**
- ○ **salt**

1. Crush the 3 kinds of peppercorn together with a pestle and mortar. Oil the roast and roll it in the pepper, pressing with the palm of your hand.
2. Heat the rotisserie. Put the roast on the spit above a roasting pan and cook for 30 minutes for medium-cooked meat.
3. Meanwhile, prepare the sauce: peel the shallots, chop very finely, and place in a small saucepan over a low heat with 20g (¾ oz) butter. When the shallots are transparent (about 5 minutes), add the cream and, as soon as it begins to boil, add the mustard. Salt to taste and keep the sauce warm.
4. When the roast is cooked, sprinkle with armagnac, using a ladle with a long handle. On contact with the heat, the alcohol will burst into flames.
5. Turn off the heat. Place the roast on a cutting board. Add 5ml (1 tsp) water to the drippings in the pan and bring to the boil, scraping up the crusty bits with a spoon. Add to the sauce.
6. Slice the roast and arrange on a hot serving dish. Heat the sauce until it bubbles and turn off the heat. Add the remaining butter while beating with a fork. Pour the sauce into a sauceboat through a fine strainer and add the juice drained from the meat while cutting. Serve immediately.

Serve this roast with Yorkshire pudding, gratinéed potatoes or cheese fritters.

Rôti à l'Ail en Chemise

Rump Roast with Garlic

Serves 8. Preparation: 5 min Cooking: 50 min
★

- ○ **1.5kg (3¼ lb) rump steak**
- ○ **1 head garlic**
- ○ **2 sprigs rosemary**
- ○ **45ml (3 tbls) oil**
- ○ **salt and pepper**

1. Ask the butcher to cut the rump steak in one piece and to bind it round to obtain a slab about 6cm (2½ inches) thick.
2. Separate the cloves from the head of garlic, remove the fine external skin but do not peel them. Make a small cut along the length of each clove with a small pointed knife.
3. Heat the oil in a sauté pan and lightly brown the meat for 5 minutes on each side, over a high heat. Then lower the heat as much as possible, salt the meat, surround it with cloves of garlic and sprigs of rosemary and cook for 25 minutes (rare) to 40 minutes (medium), turning every 10 minutes. Use two spatulas to turn the meat without piercing it.
4. When the roast is cooked, arrange on a serving dish. Untie the string and place the garlic cloves around the meat. Discard three-quarters of the cooking fat, add 100ml (3½ fl oz) water to the remainder of the fat in the pan and bring to the boil quickly, scraping up the crusty bits on the bottom of the pan. Pour this juice into a sauceboat. Serve immediately.

Serve with vegetables in season, either sautéed or braised.

Entrecôte au Beurre Rouge

Serves 4. Preparation and cooking: 30 min

Rib Steak with Red Butter

★

○ **1 rib steak, 900g-1kg (2-2¼ lb)**
○ **4 shallots**
○ **15ml (1 tbls) wine vinegar**
○ **240ml (9 fl oz) red wine:**
　　Beaujolais, Cahors, Gigondas,
　　etc
○ **15ml (1 tbls) oil**
○ **100g (4 oz) butter**
○ **salt and pepper**

1. Preheat the oven to 200°C (400°F; gas mark 6). Heat the oil in a sauté pan, add 20g (¾ oz) butter and brown the steak for 5 minutes on each side, over a low heat, to avoid burning the butter.
2. When the steak is browned, add salt, place the meat on a rack above a roasting pan and allow to cook for 15 to 20 minutes, according to its thickness and to taste. When the steak is cooked, leave it in the turned-off oven for 10 minutes.
3. 10 minutes before serving the meat, prepare the red butter in the sauté pan. Discard the fat from the roasting pan. Peel the shallots, chop them very finely and add them to the pan with the caramelized juices from the meat. Add the vinegar and place the pan over a medium heat. Allow the vinegar to boil until it evaporates, then add the wine and boil over a high heat until only 100ml (3½ fl oz) remains. Add salt and pepper. Take the pan off the heat and allow to cool for 1 minute before adding the butter, cut into small pieces, stirring with a spatula until the mixture is creamy. If the pan is too hot the butter will melt and prevent the mixture becoming creamy.
4. Remove the steak from the oven, cut it into thin slices crosswise, arrange in its original shape on a serving dish and coat with the red butter which has been passed through a strainer.

Aloyau Jardinière

Serves 4. Preparation and cooking: 20 min

Sirloin with Tomatoes and Olives

 ★★

○ **4 red, ripe tomatoes**
○ **60ml (4 tbls) oil**
○ **2 cloves garlic, sliced**
○ **4 slices sirloin, 150g (7 oz) each**
○ **salt and pepper**
○ **70g (3 oz) black olives**
○ **2 peppers in oil, sliced**
○ **1 stick celery, sliced**
○ **small handful oregano**
○ **30ml (2 tbls) vinegar**

1. Immerse the tomatoes in boiling water for 10 seconds. Peel them, halve them, remove the seeds and cut into slices. Pour the oil into a large frying pan and lightly brown the sliced garlic. Add meat slices and brown on both sides over a low heat. Season.
2. Add the pitted olives, sliced peppers, celery and tomatoes, and cook over a high heat, turning the meat a few times.
3. Sprinkle with oregano, baste with vinegar and leave to cook. When ready, place the meat and the vegetables on a hot serving dish and serve at once.

A delicious roast for 12 to 15 people can be made with a rib steak weighing 2.5kg (5½ lb). This cut is marbled and soft so it is not necessary to oil it or bard it before putting it in the oven, just tie it round and place the meat in a very hot oven, gradually lowering the heat to obtain perfect results. The meat can be punctured, like a leg of lamb, and garlic slivers with salt and pepper, sprigs of thyme and rosemary inserted. If there are 24 or more guests and if you have a very large oven, make a sumptuous roast with several ribs of beef on the bone prepared as above.

Tournedos Farcis
Stuffed Tournedos

Serves 4. Preparation: 15 min Cooking: 15 min

★★

○ **4 tournedos, 150g (5 oz) each, not barded**
○ **2 slices raw ham**
○ **150g (5 oz) Gruyère cheese**
○ **12 pitted green olives**
○ **12 medium-sized mushrooms**
○ **juice of ½ lemon**
○ **100ml (3½ fl oz) Pineau des Charentes (an aperitif)**
○ **45ml (3 tbls) double cream**
○ **30g (1¼ oz) butter**
○ **15ml (1 tbls) oil**
○ **salt and pepper**

1. Make a horizontal slit in the middle of each tournedos, without cutting right through the meat. Cut the cheese into 4 slices, slightly smaller than the tournedos. Cut 4 pieces of ham the same size as the tournedos. Slip both ham and cheese into the steaks. Chop the remainder of the ham, with its fat, finely.
2. Cut the olives into small rounds. Trim off the earthy base of the mushrooms, wash and drain them and cut them into very fine slivers. Sprinkle with lemon juice to prevent them changing colour.
3. Tie the steaks up crosswise like a parcel, salt them and pepper them lightly. Heat the oil in a frying pan, add the butter; as soon as it melts, sauté the steaks over a very low heat, to allow the cheese to melt, 2 or 3 minutes each side, depending on their thickness.
4. When the steaks are cooked, remove them from the pan, cover and keep warm.
5. Add the chopped ham to the pan, brown lightly for 1 minute, then add the drained mushrooms and increase the heat. After about 3 minutes, when the mushrooms no longer give out water, add the olives, the Pineau des Charentes and the cream. Add salt and pepper and leave to reduce for 1 minute. Return the steaks and their juices to the pan, reheat them for 30 seconds, turning once, then arrange them on a hot serving dish, coat with their sauce and serve.

Paupiettes de Boeuf
Beef Olives with Anchovies

Serves 4. Preparation and cooking: 50 min

★★

○ **8 slices chuck steak**
○ **3 hard-boiled eggs**
○ **3 red, ripe tomatoes**
○ **200g (7 oz) minced beef**
○ **50g (2 oz) breadcrumbs**
○ **6 anchovy fillets**
○ **salt and pepper**
○ **50g (2 oz) butter**
○ **150ml (5 fl oz) white wine**
○ **150ml (5 fl oz) beef stock**
○ **150ml (5 fl oz) single cream**

1. Pound the meat slices to flatten them as much as possible. Immerse the tomatoes into boiling water for 10 seconds, drain, peel, remove the seeds and chop roughly.
2. Place the mince, finely chopped hard-boiled eggs, tomatoes, breadcrumbs, finely chopped anchovy fillets, and a pinch each of salt and pepper into a bowl. Mix carefully until well blended, then divide into 8 equal parts and arrange in the middle of each slice of meat. Roll the slices up, having folded the side edges inwards to prevent the mixture escaping during cooking. Bind the rolls with white thread.
3. Melt the butter in a frying pan, add the beef olives and brown on all sides. Sprinkle with white wine and, when this has evaporated, add the hot stock and salt and pepper to taste. Allow to cook for about 25 to 30 minutes, turning often.
4. When cooked, place the beef olives on a serving dish. Add the cream to the contents remaining in the pan, bring to the boil and let thicken. Pour this over the beef olives and serve immediately.

Sirloin with Tomatoes and Olives (p21) ▶

Escalopes à la Pizzaiola
Escalopes with Wine and Anchovies

Serves 4. Preparation and cooking: 40 min

★ ★

- ○ **500g (18 oz) chuck steak or thin flank, sliced**
- ○ **flour**
- ○ **40g (1¾ oz) butter**
- ○ **salt and pepper**
- ○ **75ml (2½ fl oz) white wine**
- ○ **75ml (2½ fl oz) beef stock**
- ○ **15ml (1 tbls) tomato purée**
- ○ **30g (1¼ oz) anchovy fillets**
- ○ **30g (1¼ oz) pickled onions**
- ○ **30g (1¼ oz) pickled gherkins**
- ○ **small handful of dried oregano**

1. Lightly flatten the slices of beef with a meat pounder and sprinkle with flour.
2. Melt the butter in a large pan and place the escalopes in it. Season. Add the white wine and cook over a low heat until the wine evaporates. Add the hot stock and tomato purée and cook for 15 to 20 minutes.
3. Meanwhile, finely chop the anchovy fillets, onions, capers and gherkins and add this mixture to the meat halfway through cooking.
4. When cooked, sprinkle with the oregano and transfer the escalopes and their sauce to a serving dish. Serve immediately.

Onglet aux Échalotes Grises
Skirt Steak with Grey Shallots

Serves 4. Preparation: 20 min Cooking: 20 min

★

- ○ **4 top of skirt steaks, 180g (6 oz) each**
- ○ **16 grey shallots**
- ○ **15ml (1 tbls) oil**
- ○ **60g (2¼ oz) butter**
- ○ **salt and pepper**

1. Peel the shallots and chop finely.
2. Place a small frying pan over a gentle heat, add the shallots and sweat them for 5 minutes, turning them constantly with a spatula. Add 40g (1¾ oz) butter and brown them very gently for at least 10 minutes, turning them constantly. Add salt halfway through cooking.
3. When the shallots are cooked and lightly browned, turn off the heat and cover the pan to keep them warm.
4. Heat the oil in a large pan; add 20g (¾ oz) butter and cook the steaks over a medium heat for 3-5 minutes, depending on thickness and taste, turning them often. Arrange them on a serving dish. Discard the fat. Add 100ml (3½ fl oz) water to the dish and, scraping the bottom with a spatula, cook over a high heat until the juice is reduced to half its quantity (about 1 minute). Pour this over the steaks.
5. Spread the steaks with the shallots and the butter they were cooked in, and serve immediately.

Escalopes en Béchamel
Escalopes in White Sauce

Serves 4. Preparation: 40 min Cooking: 20 min

★

- ○ **500g (1 lb 2 oz) fillet or sirloin**
- ○ **salt and pepper**
- ○ **200ml (7 fl oz) milk**
- ○ **25g (1 oz) flour**
- ○ **80g (3¼ oz) butter**
- ○ **50g (2 oz) Parmesan cheese**
- ○ **1 truffle**

1. Slice the meat very thin, preferably using an electric slicer. Place it in a flat dish, season with salt and pepper, and sprinkle the milk over. Leave to marinate for 20 minutes, turning frequently.
2. At the end of this time, drain the slices of meat and dip them in flour several times.
3. Melt the butter in a large frying pan and add the meat. Brown lightly on both sides, then add the milk from the marinade and allow to boil until the gravy has thickened.
4. Transfer the meat slices onto a serving dish. Sprinkle with the grated Parmesan and top with very thin slices of truffle.

Foie à l'Aigre-Doux

Serves 4. Preparation: 10 min Cooking: 25 min

Sweet and Sour Liver

★

- ○ **600g (21 oz) calf's liver**
- ○ **400g (14 oz) onions**
- ○ **30ml (2 tbls) vinegar**
- ○ **30ml (2 tbls) lemon juice**
- ○ **2.5ml (½ tsp) sugar**
- ○ **5ml (1 tsp) cornflour**
- ○ **30ml (2 tbls) oil**
- ○ **60g (2¼ oz) butter**
- ○ **salt and pepper**

1. Cut the liver into very thin slices, then cut each slice into pieces 2cm (¾ inch) x 5cm (2 inches).
2. Peel the onions and cut them into very fine slivers.
3. Heat the oil in a frying pan. Add 20g (¾ oz) butter and cook the onions for about 20 minutes, until they become pale gold. Add the salt halfway through cooking. Remove from the pan and put aside.
4. Add 20g (¾ oz) butter to the pan and as soon as it melts sauté the pieces of liver very quickly over a high heat for about 3 minutes. Season halfway through cooking. Do not overcook or the liver will harden.
5. When the liver is cooked, remove from the heat. Place the liver in the dish containing the onions. Discard the fat. Mix the cornflour in a bowl with 45ml (3 tbls) cold water.
6. Put the pan back over the heat, add the vinegar and, scraping the bottom of the pan with a spatula, allow to evaporate, then add the cornflour and water mixture. Turn with a spatula until the mixture thickens, then add the sugar and lemon juice, salt and pepper; mix. Add the rest of the butter and return the liver and onions to the pan.
7. Cook for 30 seconds, turning with a spatula, then remove the pan from the heat. Serve very hot.

Serve with polenta or steamed potatoes. The dish may be sprinkled with chopped parsley, and capers and chopped gherkins may be added.

Rognons à la Moutarde

Serves 6. Preparation and cooking: 20 min

Kidneys with Mustard Sauce

★ ★

- ○ **2 calf's kidneys**
- ○ **50g (2 oz) butter**
- ○ **30ml (2 tbls) strong French mustard**
- ○ **120ml (4 fl oz) double cream**
- ○ **bunch chives, chopped**
- ○ **nutmeg**
- ○ **salt and pepper**

1. Ask your butcher to prepare the kidneys by cutting them in two, then into cubes the size of a walnut and to remove the skin and the blood vessels.
2. Melt 20g (¾ oz) butter in a saucepan, add the mustard and cream and reduce over a low heat to half their quantity, about 8 minutes.
3. Meanwhile, melt the rest of the butter in a pan, add the kidneys and sauté them for 5 to 6 minutes, depending on their thickness, over a high flame. Then add the reduced mustard sauce, season, add nutmeg to taste and allow to simmer for another 2 minutes.
4. Place the kidneys in a serving dish, sprinkle with chopped chives and serve.

Entrecôtes à la Confiture d'Oignons
Rib Steaks with Onion Sauce

Serves 4. Preparation: 20 min
Cooking: 45 min
★

○ **2 rib steaks, 500g (18 oz) each**
○ **700g (1½ lb) onions**
○ **80g (3½ oz) butter**
○ **30ml (2 tbls) granulated sugar**
○ **15ml (1 tbls) vinegar**
○ **15ml (1 tbls) oil**
○ **salt and pepper**

1. Peel the onions and mince finely. Place them in a sauté pan, sprinkle with sugar, add 60g (2¼ oz) butter, cut up, and 100ml (3½ fl oz) cold water. Heat the pan over a medium flame to boiling point. Mix, then lower the heat and cook, turning often with a spatula, until the onions are caramelized (40-45 minutes). Halfway through the cooking, add the vinegar and season to taste.
2. When the onions are cooked, cover the pan and keep warm. Heat the oil in a frying pan, add 20g (¼ oz) butter and cook the steaks for 2 minutes (rare) to 4 minutes (well done). Salt halfway through cooking.
3. Arrange the steaks on a serving dish, cover with the onion mixture and serve immediately.

Petit Sauté aux Olives de Nyons
Sautéed Steak with Black Olives

Serves 2. Preparation: 15 min
Cooking: 15 min
★

○ **500g (18 oz) sirloin or rump steak**
○ **24 black olives**
○ **20 peeled cloves of garlic**
○ **15ml (1 tbls) dried breadcrumbs**
○ **5ml (1 tsp) herbs of Provence or mixed herbs**
○ **45ml (3 tbls) olive oil**
○ **salt and pepper**

1. Cut the meat into small cubes 1.5cm (¾ inch) square.
2. Heat the oil in a small saucepan. Add the cloves of garlic and allow to cook over a low heat for about 10 minutes, until they are tender and just golden. Pour the contents of the saucepan into a frying pan large enough to hold the meat cubes without any overlapping.
3. Place the frying pan over a medium heat. As soon as the oil is hot, add the meat cubes, stirring continuously for 2 minutes, until the meat is golden brown. Then add the olives and sprinkle with herbs and breadcrumbs. Cook for 1 minute and remove from the heat. Arrange the sauté on two individual plates and serve immediately.

This Mediterranean dish may be served with *tomates à la provençale*, tomatoes stuffed with breadcrumbs, herbs and garlic, or with small potato rissoles.

Capilotade à l'Ail Nouveau
Beef with Fresh Garlic

Serves 4. Preparation: 20 min Cooking: 3½-4 hr
★

○ **1kg (2¼ lb) silverside or cheek**
○ **500g (1 lb 2 oz) ripe tomatoes**
○ **2 heads fresh garlic**
○ **2 pinches each rosemary, thyme or oregano**
○ **30ml (2 tbls) olive oil**
○ **2.5ml (½ tsp) sugar**
○ **salt and pepper**

1. Cut the meat into 2cm (¾ inch) cubes, and sprinkle with salt. Peel the garlic. Cut the tomatoes into quarters and put through a sieve or blender.
2. Heat the oil in a flameproof dish and turn the meat in it without allowing it to colour for 5 minutes. Then add the rosemary and other herbs, the cloves of garlic and the tomatoes. Season with sugar and salt. Cover the dish and leave to simmer over a low heat. Or place in the oven at 180°C (350°F; gas mark 4) for between 3 and 4 hours depending on the piece of meat chosen: cheek, which is more tender, will cook in 2½ to 3 hours.
3. The dish is ready when the meat is tender enough to fall apart easily, the cloves of garlic can be reduced to purée and the sauce has thickened up nicely. Add pepper and serve immediately.

Escalopes with Wine and Anchovies (p24) ▶

Boeuf aux Poivrons à la Chinoise

Serves 4. Preparation: 15 min
Cooking: 10 min

Beef with Peppers, Chinese Style

★ ★

○ **500g (18 oz) sirloin or rump steak**
○ **2 green peppers**
○ **1 medium-sized onion**
○ **1 piece ginger root, 3cm (1¼ inch) long**
○ **15ml (1 tbls) rice wine or sherry**
○ **45ml (3 tbls) soya sauce**
○ **2.5ml (½ tsp) sugar**
○ **5ml (1 tsp) cornflour**
○ **45ml (3 tbls) oil**

1. Ask the butcher for 1 or 2 slices of meat 4cm (1½ inches) thick. Cut each slice into rectangles 2cm (1 inch) by 4cm (1½ inches) and 3cm (1¼ inches) thick. Mix the cornflour, wine, soya sauce and sugar in a bowl. Add the slivers of beef and turn to ensure they are well covered by the mixture.
2. Wash the peppers, cut them into 4 lengthwise, remove the seeds and white filaments, and cut each quarter into fine slivers 3mm (⅛ inch) wide. Peel the onion and mince as finely as possible. Peel and grate the ginger.
3. Heat 30ml (2 tbls) oil in a wok (a Chinese pan with rounded bottom) or a deep-sided sauté pan and cook the onions for 2 minutes, until they become transparent. Add the peppers and sauté for 3 minutes, stirring often with a spatula, till they are tender but not golden. Remove the vegetables with a skimmer and put aside.
4. Add the rest of the oil to the pan and heat. Add the ginger. Stir for 3 seconds and add the meat, and sauté over a high heat for 3 minutes, until no liquid is left in the pan. Put the vegetables back, stir for 10 seconds and remove from the heat. Serve very hot.

You may add to this recipe 100g (4 oz) Chinese vermicelli cut in pieces 10cm (4 inches) long and fried briskly for several seconds, until they are lightly browned.

Faux-Filet au Beurre d'Anchois

Serves 2. Preparation: 5 min Cooking: 5-6 min

Sirloin Steaks with Anchovy Butter

★

○ **2 sirloin steaks, 200g (7 oz) each**
○ **4 anchovies in salt**
○ **15ml (1 tbls) wine vinegar**
○ **15ml (1 tbls) oil**
○ **50g (2 oz) butter**
○ **pepper**

1. Wash the anchovies in running water to remove all the grains of salt. Separate into fillets, remove the bones and cut into small cubes. Put aside on a plate.
2. Heat the oil in a frying pan. Add 20g (¾ oz) butter and cook the steaks in this over a medium heat for 1-2 minutes on each side, according to their thickness and to taste.
3. Arrange the steaks on individual plates and discard all the cooking fat from the pan. Lower the heat and add the vinegar and then the anchovies. Scrape the bottom of the pan with a spatula to detach the crusty bits from the meat, and after 30 seconds, when the anchovies have been reduced to a purée, remove the pan from the heat.
4. Away from the heat, add the rest of the butter to the pan in small pieces, turning with the spatula until the mixture becomes creamy. Pepper generously, coat the steaks with the sauce and serve immediately.

Serve with *tomates à la provencale* (tomatoes stuffed with garlic, herbs and breadcrumbs), sautéed aubergine, sautéed or battered and deep-fried onion rings.

Tournedos Rossini

Serves 4. Preparation and cooking: 30 min

Tournedos in Madeira Sauce

★ ★ ★

- ○ **4 tournedos, 150g (5 oz) each**
- ○ **4 slices bread (from a cottage loaf)**
- ○ **200g (7 oz) butter**
- ○ **salt and pepper**
- ○ **150ml (5 fl oz) Madeira**
- ○ **15ml (1 tbls) flour**
- ○ **150ml (5 fl oz) beef stock**
- ○ **4 round slices of goose liver pâté**
- ○ **4 slices black truffle**

1. Bind the tournedos to preserve their shape during cooking.
2. Cut the slices of bread to fit the tournedos, brown in 50g (2 oz) butter and keep warm.
3. Heat 100g (4 oz) butter in a large frying pan, add the tournedos and cook on both sides over a high heat for about 3 minutes. Then season, remove from the pan and keep warm on a serving dish.
4. Add the Madeira to the remaining cooking juices and bring to a boil. Mix the remaining butter with the flour and stir into the sauce, which will thicken. Dilute with the boiling Madeira mixture and allow to cook until a thick sauce is formed (about 5 minutes).
5. At this point, top each piece of bread with a tournedos, then a slice of pâté, then a slice of truffle. Pour over the Madeira sauce and serve immediately.

Tournedos à l'Anglaise

Serves 4. Preparation and cooking: 40 min

Tournedos English Style

★ ★

- ○ **300g (10 oz) cèpes (boletus mushrooms)**
- ○ **100g (4 oz) butter**
- ○ **1 clove garlic, sliced**
- ○ **100g (4 oz) cooked ham**
- ○ **salt and pepper**
- ○ **2.5ml (½ tsp) meat extract**
- ○ **4 tournedos weighing 150g (5 oz) each**

1. Scrape the cèpes with a sharp knife to remove all traces of earth, clean with a damp cloth, dry carefully and cut into thin slices.
2. Melt 50g (2 oz) butter. Add the sliced garlic and allow to colour, then add the ham, which has been roughly chopped, and allow to brown over a low heat. Then add the mushrooms, season with salt and pepper, and stir. Cook for several minutes over a high flame to evaporate any liquid. Add 75ml (2½ fl oz) lukewarm water in which the meat extract has been dissolved and allow to cook for 15-20 minutes over a low heat.
3. Shortly before the end of this time, melt the remaining butter in a pan and cook the tournedos on both sides over a high flame for 3-4 minutes. Season. Place the tournedos on a serving dish, cover with the cèpes and their sauce and serve.

Hamburgers à l'Oignon

Serves 4. Preparation: 20 min Cooking: 10 min

Hamburgers with Onions

★

- ○ **400g (14 oz) minced beef**
- ○ **1 large onion**
- ○ **2 eggs**
- ○ **salt and pepper**
- ○ **pinch nutmeg**
- ○ **15ml (1 tbls) oil**

1. Cut the onion in half. Chop one half very finely and slice the other into rings. Put the meat in a bowl and add the chopped onion, the eggs, and a pinch of salt, pepper and nutmeg.
2. Mix the ingredients together very carefully and divide the mixture into four. If you have a 'hamburger press', use it to shape the burgers, otherwise use your hands.
3. Brush both sides of the hamburgers generously with oil and cook under a very hot grill for about 10 minutes. Arrange on a heated serving dish and garnish with onion rings.

Tournedos à la Crème

Tournedos with Cream Sauce

Serves 4. Preparation and cooking: 20 min

★

- ○ **handful black peppercorns**
- ○ **salt**
- ○ **4 tournedos, 150g (5 oz) each**
- ○ **50g (2 oz) butter**
- ○ **100ml (3½ fl oz) brandy**
- ○ **120ml (4 fl oz) double cream**
- ○ **15ml (1 tbls) French mustard**

1. Pound the peppercorns roughly in a mortar, mix with a pinch of salt and press with the palms of your hands onto both sides of each tournedos.
2. Melt the butter in a frying pan and add the tournedos, letting them brown on both sides over a high flame for 2-3 minutes. Place on a dish and keep warm. Pour the brandy into the pan, allow to get hot, then set alight. As soon as the flame dies, add the cream mixed with the mustard, stir well and bring to the boil.
3. Return the tournedos to the pan, cook for a minute, then remove from the heat, place on a serving dish and serve immediately.

Entrecôtes au Vinaigre

Rib Steaks with Vinegar

Serves 2. Preparation: 5 min Cooking: 5 min

★

- ○ **2 rib steaks, 200g (7 oz) each**
- ○ **2 small sprigs rosemary**
- ○ **6 cloves garlic**
- ○ **30ml (2 tbls) wine vinegar**
- ○ **30ml (2 tbls) olive oil**
- ○ **salt and pepper**

1. Peel the garlic. Heat the oil in a pan large enough to contain both steaks.
2. When the oil is hot, place the steaks in the pan with the garlic and rosemary sprigs and cook over a medium heat, for 1-2 minutes on each side, depending on whether you want the meat rare or well done. Don't forget to turn the garlic cloves as well.
3. When the steaks are done, arrange them on individual plates and pour the vinegar into the pan, scraping the bottom with a spatula to deglaze it. When the vinegar boils, put the steaks back in the pan, salt and pepper them, turn them after 10 seconds, season the other side, and after another 10 seconds remove the pan from the heat.
4. Put the steaks back on the plates, pour the sauce over them, surround them with the browned garlic cloves and rosemary sprigs and serve immediately.

Here is another version of this recipe: substitute 3 finely chopped shallots for the garlic cloves; substitute thyme for the rosemary, and replace the olive oil with 40g (1¾ oz) butter. Accompany these delicious steaks with gratinéed potatoes, cauliflower or courgettes.

Steak Mariné

Marinated Steak

Serves 4. Preparation: 30 min Cooking: 10 min

★

- ○ **8 100g (4 oz) slices sirloin or fillet steak**
- ○ **90ml (6 tbls) oil**
- ○ **juice of 1 lemon**
- ○ **salt and pepper**
- ○ **marjoram**

1. Pour the oil into a dish. Add the lemon juice, a pinch of salt and a dash of pepper. Beat this mixture with a fork and put the meat into it. Leave to marinate for about 20 to 30 minutes (during this time, turn the meat frequently to make sure it absorbs as much marinade as possible).
2. Heat the grill and cook the slices of meat on both sides under a high heat. Then arrange on a serving dish. Pour a little of the marinade over, and garnish with a handful of marjoram. Serve at once.

This dish should be eaten very hot.

Boeuf Stroganoff

Serves 4. Preparation: 30 min Cooking: 25 min

Beef Stroganoff

★★

- ○ **600g (21 oz) fillet steak**
- ○ **4 medium-sized onions**
- ○ **400g (14 oz) button mushrooms**
- ○ **200ml (7 fl oz) double cream**
- ○ **15ml (1 tbls) lemon juice**
- ○ **15ml (1 tbls) strong French mustard**
- ○ **30ml (2 tbls) oil**
- ○ **40g (1¾ oz) butter**
- ○ **salt and pepper**

1. Since the meat has to be cut into fine strips, buy the rib end of fillet as it is much cheaper than the middle cuts and just as tender.
2. Cut the meat into slices ½cm (¼ inch) thick, then into strips 2cm (1 inch) by 3cm (1¼ inches).
3. Peel the onions and cut them into fine rounds. Trim the earthy base off the mushrooms, wash and drain them. Mix the mustard, lemon juice and cream in a bowl.
4. In a sauté pan, heat 15ml (1 tbls) oil, add half the butter and lightly brown the onion rounds over a low heat for about 10 minutes, until they are golden.
5. Meanwhile, cut the mushrooms in fine strips and, as soon as the onions are golden, add them to the pan. Increase the heat and allow to cook for about 10 minutes, until the mushrooms no longer give out any liquid and are browning gently. Then add the cream mixture and salt and pepper to taste. Reduce to half the quantity (about 5 minutes).
6. Meanwhile, heat the rest of the oil in a frying pan and add the remaining butter and the fillet. Fry the meat briskly over a high flame for 2 minutes, until it no longer gives out any liquid. Then pour the meat and its juices into the sauté pan containing the mushrooms and onions, stir for 30 seconds, remove from the heat, pour everything onto a hot dish and serve immediately.

Entrecôtes Marchand de Vin

Serves 4. Preparation: 5 min Cooking: 15 min

Rib Steaks with Red Wine Sauce

★

- ○ **2 rib steaks, 450g (1 lb) each**
- ○ **4 grey shallots, finely chopped**
- ○ **240ml (9 fl oz) red wine**
- ○ **15ml (1 tbls) oil**
- ○ **120g (4½ oz) butter**
- ○ **15ml (1 tbls) lemon juice**
- ○ **5ml (1 tsp) chopped parsley**
- ○ **10ml (2 tsp) freshly ground pepper**
- ○ **salt**

1. Heat the oil in a frying pan, add 20g (¾ oz) butter and cook the steaks over a low heat, for 3 or 4 minutes each side, depending on whether you want the steaks rare or well done.
2. When the steaks are ready, place on a serving dish and keep warm in a lukewarm oven (not lit) or placed over a saucepan of boiling water.
3. Discard the fat left in the pan. Add the shallots and red wine to the pan, scraping the bottom of the pan with a spatula to detach crusty bits, then add pepper and salt to taste and allow the wine to reduce to one-quarter of its original volume, over a high heat, for about 5 minutes.
4. When the wine has reduced, add the lemon juice, the juice from the meat, and the parsley. Mix and remove from the heat.
5. Away from the heat, add the remaining butter to the pan in small pieces, mixing with a spatula until it is creamy, then pour this sauce over the steaks and serve immediately.

To make steaks à la Bordelaise (with red wine and marrow sauce), use Bordeaux wine and add 1 sprig of thyme and ½ bay leaf, then strain the sauce through a fine strainer and add 50g (2 oz) marrow, cut into small cubes and poached for 3 minutes in salted water.

Bavette à la Moutarde

Serves 4. Preparation: 5 min Cooking: 10-15 min

Top of Sirloin with Mustard Sauce

★

○ **700g (1½ lb) top of sirloin in one piece**
○ **30ml (2 tbls) strong French mustard**
○ **180ml (6 fl oz) double cream**
○ **50ml (1¾ fl oz) dry white vermouth**
○ **2 sprigs tarragon**
○ **5ml (1 tsp) freeze-dried green peppercorns**
○ **15ml (1 tbls) oil**
○ **20g (¾ oz) butter**
○ **salt**

1. Ask the butcher for the meat in one piece, of an even thickness, if possible. With a knife, make small perpendicular incisions in the fibres of the meat to prevent swelling during cooking.
2. Wash and dry the tarragon and chop the leaves. Crush the green peppercorns between your fingers.
3. Heat the oil in a frying pan large enough to hold the meat, add the butter and brown the meat over a medium flame. According to the thickness of the meat and to taste, cook from 3 to 6 minutes on each side. Salt halfway through the cooking.
4. When the meat is cooked, take it out of the pan and place on a serving dish. Discard all the fat left in the pan, add the vermouth and cook over a high flame, scraping up the crusty bits on the bottom of the pan. As soon as the vermouth has evaporated add the cream and green peppercorns. Allow the cream to reduce to half its quantity for 3 minutes over a high flame, then add the mustard and allow to boil for 30 seconds, add the tarragon and stir. Return the meat to the pan, adding any juices which have accumulated, and cook for 10 seconds on each side, then remove from the pan, place on the serving dish and coat with the sauce. Serve immediately.

Steaks aux Câpres

Serves 4. Preparation: 15 min Cooking: 10 min

Steaks with Capers

★

○ **4 steaks, 150g (5 oz)-180g (6 oz) each: sirloin, fillet, flank or rib steak**
○ **60ml (4 tbls) capers**
○ **24 black olives in brine (kalamatas)**
○ **4 medium-sized ripe tomatoes**
○ **2 pinches oregano**
○ **30ml (2 tbls) olive oil**
○ **salt**

1. Pit and dice the olives. Drain the capers thoroughly by pressing them in the palm of your hand. Immerse the tomatoes in boiling water for 10 seconds, rinse under cold water, cut into halves, remove the seeds and chop roughly.
2. Heat the oil in a frying pan and cook the meat for 30 seconds to 2 minutes on each side, according to its thickness and to taste.
3. When the steaks are cooked, remove them from the pan and keep them warm on a serving dish placed over a saucepan containing boiling water. Add the tomatoes to the pan and cook for 5 minutes over a high flame, until they have let out almost all their liquid. Then lightly salt them, sprinkle with oregano, add the capers and olives, mix, cook everything for 1 minute and return the steaks to the pan, together with their juice, just long enough to reheat them.
4. Arrange the steaks on a serving dish, coat them with the sauce and serve immediately.

Accompany these steaks with sautéed aubergine or grilled peppers. You can vary the sauce by adding 5ml (1 tsp) anchovy paste and 1 small red pepper, chopped.

Steaks au Poivre

Serves 4. Preparation: 5 min Cooking: 10 min

Pepper Steaks

★★

○ **4 steaks (rump or fillet), 200g (7 oz) each**
○ **60ml (4 tbls) freshly ground pepper**
○ **60ml (4 tbls) Fine Champagne cognac**
○ **60ml (4 tbls) double cream**
○ **40g (1¾ oz) butter**
○ **salt**

1. Pour half the cognac into a dish and place the pepper on a plate.
2. Dip both sides of the steaks into the cognac, then into the pepper, pressing with your palm to make the pepper stick. Salt the steaks and allow to marinate for 15 minutes.
3. Then melt the butter in a frying pan and lightly brown the steaks for 2 to 3 minutes on each side, depending on whether you like them rare or well done.
4. When the steaks are ready, sprinkle with the rest of the cognac, set them alight, remove from the pan and place on a warmed serving dish.
5. Discard the butter, and add half the cream to the pan. Reduce for 1 minute over a high flame, while scraping the bottom of the pan to deglaze it and detach all the meat juices, then add the rest of the cream, boil for 10 seconds, mix, pour over the steaks and serve immediately.

Accompany these pepper steaks with potatoes cut into matchstick-sized strips and sautéed, and bunches of cress. 5ml (1 tsp) strong French mustard can be added to the pan with the cream, Armagnac or ordinary Cognac can replace the Fine Champagne cognac.

Joue de Boeuf à la Bière Blonde

Serves 4-5. Preparation: 20 min
Cooking: 3 hr 30 min

Ox Cheek in Pale Ale

★

○ **1kg (2¼ lb) ox cheek**
○ **1kg (2¼ lb) leeks (the white part only)**
○ **½ litre (18 fl oz) pale ale**
○ **15ml (1 tbls) oil**
○ **50g (2 oz) butter**
○ **5ml (1 tsp) sugar**
○ **salt and pepper**

1. Ox cheek is an extremely tender cut of meat, very suitable for braising since it is quick to cook and has a most delicate flavour. Cut it into 2cm (¾ inch) cubes, and season with salt.
2. You will need more than 2kg (4½ lb) of unprepared leeks to obtain 1kg (2¼ lb) of the white part only. Peel and wash them, and then weigh to make sure you have equal weights of leeks and meat. Cut across into slices ½cm (1/6 inch) thick.
3. Heat the oil in a heavy pan, add some of the butter and brown the pieces of meat for about 5 minutes over a gentle heat; then remove with a slotted spoon.
4. Add the rest of the butter and the leeks to the pan. Sweat the leeks over a low heat for about 5 minutes making sure they do not brown, and add the sugar, salt and pepper. Return the meat and pour in the ale up to halfway. Bring to the boil, then lower the heat, cover, and leave to stew over a very low heat for about 2 hours 30 minutes till the meat is tender. If at the end of that time a lot of juice remains uncover the pan and let it reduce until only a syrupy residue is left to coat the meat and vegetables. Serve hot.

Accompany with gratinéed potatoes.

Beef with Golden Eggs (p48) ▶

Boeuf Bourguignon

Beef Burgundy Style

Serves 8. Preparation: 45 min Cooking: 4 hr

★★

- ○ **1.8kg (4 lb) beef: ⅓ rump, ⅓ silverside, ⅓ chuck**
- ○ **1 litre (1¾ pints) red Burgundy wine**
- ○ **250g (9 oz) bacon**
- ○ **36 small onions**
- ○ **36 small button mushrooms**
- ○ **30ml (2 tbls) marc or cognac**
- ○ **10ml (2 tsp) cornflour or arrowroot**
- ○ **50g (2 oz) butter**
- ○ **15ml (1 tbls) oil**
- ○ **juice of ½ lemon**
- ○ **salt and pepper**

1. Peel the onions. Cut the bacon into sticks 1cm (½ inch) across. Cut the meat into cubes 4cm (1½ inches) square, and season.
2. Bring to the boil 2 litres (3½ pints) water in a saucepan, immerse the bacon sticks and blanch for 5 minutes, drain.
3. Heat the oil in a large stewpan and lightly brown the bacon sticks over a low heat for about 8 minutes, till the bacon fat is transparent. Remove with a skimmer and put aside in a bowl.
4. Add 20g (¾ oz) butter to the pan and add the onions. Lightly brown over a low heat for about 15 minutes. Remove with a skimmer and add to the bacon.
5. Add several of the cubes of beef to the pan and brown lightly (about 5 minutes), then remove and put aside. Repeat until all the meat is browned. Then discard the fat from cooking and pour the wine into the pan while scraping up the crusty bits with a spatula. Bring the wine to the boil, set alight, and when the flame is extinguished, return the beef to the pan. Bring back to the boil, cover and simmer over a very low heat, without boiling, for about 4 hours.
6. After 3 hours, add the bacon sticks and onions. Trim the earthy base off the mushrooms, wash, wipe and place in a sauté pan with the lemon juice and the remainder of the butter. Brown over a high heat until they give out no more liquid and are lightly browned, then add the mushrooms and their juices to the stew.
7. After about 4 hours, when the meat is almost tender, pour the contents of the stewpan into a saucepan through a strainer. Return the contents of the strainer to the stewpan and cover. Allow the sauce to stand for 5 minutes, then skim off the fat with a spoon.
8. Dilute the cornflour or arrowroot with 30ml (2 tbls) cold water and pour the mixture into the saucepan, stirring with a wooden spoon. Bring the sauce to the boil, then heat the marc or cognac in a small saucepan, set alight and add to the sauce. Boil over a high heat until the sauce thickens enough to coat the spoon and reduce until just enough is left to cover the pieces of meat (5 to 10 minutes). Add salt and pepper to taste, pour into the stewpan and simmer for 10 minutes, then serve immediately.

Boeuf Bourguignon should be served very hot on hot plates, accompanied by steamed or gratinéed potatoes. This dish is best when prepared with a large quantity of meat and better still when reheated: so prepare two meals at once, one to serve tonight and one to refrigerate.

In former times, a whole side of beef rump steak was prepared à la bourguignonne. *Try making it with a piece of rump steak weighing 1.6kg (3½ lb), larded and bound by the butcher. After the wine has been added to the stewpan, cover and cook in a preheated oven for 4 hours at 140°C (275°F; gas mark 1).*

Grillade des Mariniers

Sailor's Grill

*Serves 6-7. Preparation: 30 min
Cooking: 3½-4 hr Marinade: 24 hr*
★ ★

- ○ **1.5kg (3¼ lb) beef flank or silverside**
- ○ **1kg (2¼ lb) onions**
- ○ **4 cloves garlic**
- ○ **90ml (6 tbls) olive oil**
- ○ **30ml (2 tbls) wine vinegar**
- ○ **1 strip orange peel, 3cm (1¼ inches) long**
- ○ **1 bay leaf**
- ○ **2 cloves**
- ○ **nutmeg**
- ○ **4 anchovies in salt**
- ○ **salt and pepper**

1. The day before: ask the butcher to cut the meat into slices weighing 100-120g (4-4½ oz), ½cm (¼ inch) thick. Trim them. Mix the vinegar, 60ml (4 tbls) olive oil, salt, pepper and nutmeg to taste in a dish. Beat until the mixture becomes creamy. Place the beef slices in a bowl, cover with the marinade and add the cloves, chopped bay leaf and orange peel. Cover and refrigerate overnight.
2. The next day: peel 3 cloves of garlic, put them through a press and collect the juice in a bowl. Peel the onions, mince very finely, add to the bowl with the garlic, salt and a little pepper, and mix.
3. Oil an earthenware dish or a cast-iron pot with 15ml (1 tbls) olive oil. Put in a layer of onions, without overlapping them, then a layer of meat slices, also without overlapping. Continue in this way, alternating the layers of onions and meat, and finishing with a layer of onions.
4. Pour the sauce over this last layer, discarding the orange peel, cloves and bay leaf, seal the pan with a piece of oiled greaseproof paper under the lid and cook over a low heat for at least 3 hours, until the juice rises to the surface, the meat is tender and the onions soft. The dish can also be cooked in the oven at 140°C (275°F; gas mark 1).
5. When the meat is cooked, peel the last clove of garlic and wash and separate the anchovies. Place the anchovies and garlic into a mortar, pound to a cream, add the final spoonful of oil and 2 spoonfuls of juice from the pan. Mix well, pour over the meat, allow to simmer for 2 minutes and serve from the cooking dish.

This onion and anchovy stew, a very old Provençal recipe, was carried on journeys by Rhône boatmen, ready to be reheated. It is called a 'grill' because the meat is cut like steak. This dish is excellent reheated: the larger the quantity of meat prepared the better.

Stews, although they take a long time, only require to be 'launched' as from then on they look after themselves. Nowadays slow-cooking pots are available with thermostats to regulate the cooking. Stews and simmered dishes can be cooked without constant surveillance.

Estouffade au Cidre

Serves 6. Preparation: 30 min Cooking: 4 hr

Beef with Cider

★ ★

- ○ **1.5kg (3¼ lb) beef: ⅓ chuck, ⅓ blade, ⅓ silverside**
- ○ **750ml (1 bottle) rough cider**
- ○ **50ml (1¾ fl oz) Calvados**
- ○ **150ml (5 fl oz) cider vinegar**
- ○ **30 shallots**
- ○ **250g (9 oz) carrots**
- ○ **150g (5 oz) pork rind**
- ○ **1 bouquet garni consisting of: 1 sprig thyme, 1 bay leaf, 4 sprigs parsley**
- ○ **45ml (3 tbls) oil**
- ○ **75g (3 oz) butter**
- ○ **salt and pepper**
- ○ **6 green golden delicious apples**

1. Cut the meat into cubes 3cm (1¼ inches) square. Peel the shallots and carrots. Cut the carrots into 4 lengthwise, then cut each stick into 2, removing the centre pith if the carrots are old.
2. Boil some water in a saucepan. Cut the pork rind into strips 1cm (½ inch) by 2cm (¾ inch). When water boils plunge in the pork strips, blanch for 5 minutes, then drain and put aside.
3. Heat some oil in a sauté pan. Seal the meat cubes over a high flame for 3-4 minutes, until they are lightly browned, then remove from the pan with a skimmer and drop into a stewpan large enough to contain the meat, vegetables and cider.
4. Add 25g (1 oz) butter to the sauté pan and, when melted, sauté the carrots and shallots for 5 minutes without allowing them to brown.
5. Meanwhile, place the stewpan over a low heat and sprinkle the meat with Calvados, then set alight while turning with a spatula. When the flame has died, add the carrots, shallots, bouquet garni and salt to taste.
6. Discard the oil remaining in the sauté pan, then pour in the vinegar and cider. When the liquid boils, pour into the stewpan. Cover and leave to cook very gently for 4 hours, placing an asbestos mat under the pan if necessary. The liquid should barely simmer.
7. ¼ hour before the end of cooking, peel and quarter the apples, remove the core and pips, then cut each quarter into 3 or 4 strips 1cm (½ inch) thick, according to the size of the apples. Melt 50g (2 oz) butter in a very large frying pan and quickly sauté the apples over a high flame until they become caramelized. Turn gently with a spatula to lightly brown both sides while cooking, which will take 6-8 minutes.
8. When the meat is cooked, pour all the juices into a saucepan and reduce over a high flame to a third of its original volume. It will acquire a syrupy consistency. Add to the meat. Allow to simmer for 2 minutes, then add pepper to taste, pour into a serving dish, removing the bouquet garni. Serve immediately, with the apples separately.

Well-iced rough cider is an excellent accompaniment to this stew.

Long cooking, necessary to obtain soft and tender meat, will never tenderize dry, fibrous meat which comes from an old animal; on the contrary, the defects will become even more evident during cooking. But meat from very young animals is no good either: it will have no taste and the juices will be too light. Be advised by your butcher and choose pieces to braise taken from animals between 3 and 6 years old.

Goulash (p46) ▶

Alouettes sans Tête

Serves 6. Preparation: 30 min Cooking: 2 hr 15 min

Beef Olives in Tomato Sauce

★★

○ **12 top of sirloin or round steaks, 100g (4 oz) each**
○ **120g (4½ oz) mild-cure bacon**
○ **2 cloves garlic**
○ **45ml (3 tbls) chopped parsley**
○ **1kg (2¼ lb) red, ripe tomatoes**
○ **150ml (5 fl oz) dry white wine**
○ **45ml (3 tbls) oil**
○ **2 medium-sized onions**
○ **nutmeg**
○ **salt and pepper**

1. Peel and chop onions finely. Wash the tomatoes, cut into 4, pass through a mincer and put the purée aside.
2. Peel the garlic and chop finely. Discard the rind of the bacon; chop the remainder as finely as possible. Mix the bacon, garlic and parsley. Pepper generously.
3. Spread the centre of each steak with this mixture and roll up. Bind each end with white thread.
4. Heat the oil in a stewpan and seal the beef olives for about 5 minutes over a high flame without allowing them to brown. Then add the onions, lightly brown for 2 minutes, and add the white wine. Lower the heat and allow the wine to evaporate completely while turning the meat rolls constantly. Then add the purée of tomatoes, salt, pepper and nutmeg to taste, cover the stewpan and allow to simmer for at least 2 hours, until meat is tender and sauce syrupy. Correct seasoning, untie the meat rolls and serve.

Serve this dish with noodles with butter and grated cheese.

Carbonades Flamandes

Serves 4. Preparation: 25 min Cooking: 3 hr

Beef and Onions Braised in Beer

★

○ **1.2kg (2½ lb) beef: chuck, rump or blade**
○ **400g (14 oz) onions**
○ **1 slice white bread, crusts removed**
○ **15ml (1 tbls) strong Dijon mustard**
○ **300ml (10 fl oz) beer, brown preferably**
○ **1 clove garlic**
○ **5ml (1 tsp) sugar**
○ **30ml (2 tbls) wine vinegar**
○ **45ml (3 tbls) oil**
○ **1 bay leaf**
○ **salt and pepper**

1. Ask the butcher to cut the meat into slices 1cm (½ inch) thick. Cut these into strips 4cm (1½ inches) by 6cm (2½ inches). Salt and pepper them. Peel and finely chop the onions. Peel the garlic and chop very finely.
2. Preheat the oven to 120°C (250°F; gas mark ½). Heat the oil in a sauté pan and seal the meat slices over a high flame without browning. Remove from the pan and reserve. Add the onions to the pan and cook over a medium heat until transparent, about 5 minutes, then sprinkle with sugar, add the vinegar, mix and remove from the heat.
3. Place alternate layers of meat and onions in a stewpan or earthenware ovenproof dish. Place in the centre a slice of bread spread with the mustard. Break the bay leaf in half and put half on each side of the bread. Push the bread down well.
4. Heat the beer in the sauté pan and then pour over the meat and onions. It should not cover the meat. Cover the dish and cook in the oven for 3 hours. When the meat is tender, remove from the stewpan or dish, arrange the slices in a deep serving dish, cover and keep warm in the turned-off oven. Purée the sauce, bread and onions in a vegetable mill, and pour over the meat. Serve immediately.

Accompany this stew with chipped or steamed potatoes. This dish can also be cooked on top of the stove over a low heat for 4 hours. In this case, crumble the bread and cut the meat into large cubes.

Compote de Gîte-Gîte au Poivre

Serves 6. Preparation: 10 min
Cooking: 5 hr
★

Brisket Stew with Pepper

○ **1.5kg (3¼ lb) brisket**
○ **750ml (1 bottle) red wine**
○ **20g (¾ oz) coarsely ground pepper**
○ **3 ripe tomatoes, peeled, seeded and crushed**
○ **2 cloves garlic**
○ **50g (2 oz) butter**
○ **salt**

1. It is important to use this gelatinous part of the beef which will become, after long, gentle cooking, tender and succulent. Cut the meat into cubes 2cm (¾ inch) square. Put them in a stewpan and add salt to taste and the crushed tomatoes.
2. Peel the garlic cloves, crush them with the palm of your hand on a board, and add to the meat. Barely cover with water, and add the butter cut into small pieces. Cover with the lid and allow to simmer over a very low heat.
3. After 2 hours, remove the lid, add 150ml (5 fl oz) wine and 15ml (1 tbls) pepper to the stewpan. Repeat this five times – every 30 minutes – until no wine or pepper remains, then cook for a further 30 minutes or longer until the stew is done. When cooked, allow to cool slightly before serving for even better results.

Accompany this dish with buttered noodles or with roughly mashed potatoes, with butter and grated cheese.

Compote aux Pommes de Terre

Serves 6. Preparation: 25 min Cooking: 3 hr
★

Beef Stew with Potatoes

○ **1kg (2¼ lb) chuck or cheek**
○ **1kg (2¼ lb) floury potatoes**
○ **1kg (2¼ lb) ripe tomatoes**
○ **45ml (3 tbls) olive oil**
○ **salt and pepper**

1. Cut the meat into 2cm (¾ inch) cubes and season with salt. Peel and dice the potatoes into 2cm (¾ inch) pieces. Wash and quarter the tomatoes, put them through a sieve or blender.
2. Preheat the oven to 195°C (375°F; gas mark 5). Grease an ovenproof dish with 15ml (1 tbls) of oil. Put in the meat, potatoes and tomato purée. Mix together well and season to taste. Pour in 15ml (1 tbls) of oil, cover the dish and place in the oven for 3 hours.
3. At the end of this time, the meat should be tender enough to part easily, and the potatoes reduced to a purée. If not, leave to cook for a further 30 minutes. Add a generous seasoning of pepper and the last 15ml (1 tbls) of oil before serving.

To seal a stewpan with luting: work 200g (7 oz) flour with 100ml (3½ fl oz) water. Form the paste into a sausage shape and press this around the edge of the lid of the stewpan, then place the lid on the pan and press together. It is a good idea to do this when you are cooking a stew for several hours.

Pièce de Boeuf à la Purée d'Aubergines
Pot Roast with Aubergines

Serves 6-7. Preparation: 40 min
Cooking: 3½-4 hr
★★

- ○ 1 roast, 1.5kg (3¼ lb), larded and bound by the butcher: rump, flank or topside
- ○ 1.5kg (3¼ lb) aubergines
- ○ 2 medium-sized onions
- ○ 1 red or green pepper
- ○ 500g (18 oz) tomatoes, peeled, seeded and crushed
- ○ 1 clove of garlic
- ○ 45ml (3 tbls) olive oil
- ○ 5ml (1 tsp) granulated sugar
- ○ salt and pepper

1. Peel the aubergines and cut them into cubes 1.5cm (¾ inch) square. Put them in a colander, sprinkle with 15ml (1 tbls) salt and leave to sweat for 30 minutes. Peel the garlic; peel and chop the onions. Wash the pepper, cut into 4, remove the core, seeds and white filaments, then cut into small cubes.
2. Heat the oil in an oval pan a little longer than the roast and brown the meat on all sides over a medium heat for about 10 minutes, then remove the meat from the pan and add the onions and pepper. Cook over a low heat for about 10 minutes, until the onion is transparent, then turn off the heat and put the meat back in the pan.
3. Preheat the oven to 170°C (325°F; gas mark 3). Wash the aubergines and wipe them dry. Place them around the meat, sprinkle them with sugar and place the tomatoes on top. Add salt, seal the pan with luting and place in the oven.
4. Leave to cook for 3½ to 4 hours, depending on the cut of meat chosen. When the meat is tender enough for a knife point to pierce it easily, remove it from the pan. Pass the vegetables through a vegetable mill or liquidize them to make a purée. Season with salt and pepper.
5. Remove the string from the meat and place on a serving dish. Pour the aubergine purée into a bowl and serve.

If there are any leftovers, serve them cold with lemon quarters, olive oil and slices of wholemeal bread.

Queue au Céleri
Oxtail with Celery

Serves 6. Preparation: 20 min Cooking: 3 hr 45 min
★★

- ○ 2 oxtails cut into pieces 4cm (1½ inches) long
- ○ 2 heads celery
- ○ 240ml (9 fl oz) white wine
- ○ 1kg (2¼ lb) ripe tomatoes
- ○ 1 medium-sized onion
- ○ 1 medium-sized carrot
- ○ 1 clove garlic
- ○ 50g (2 oz) mild-cure bacon
- ○ 30ml (2 tbls) oil
- ○ salt and pepper

1. Peel the onion, carrot and garlic and mince together. Chop the bacon. Wash and quarter the tomatoes, and pass them through a vegetable mill. Put the resulting juice aside.
2. Heat the oil in a stewpan and add the oxtail, chopped bacon and vegetable mixture. Cook for about 5 minutes over a medium heat, without allowing them to brown, then add the wine and allow it to evaporate, stirring constantly with a spatula. Add salt and pepper to taste.
3. When the wine has evaporated, add the tomato juice to the pan, then add water to completely cover the meat. As soon as it boils, cover the pan, lower the heat and allow to simmer over a very low heat for about 3½ hours, until the meat comes away from the bones and is very tender.
4. Halfway through the cooking, wash and trim the celery and slice into pieces 6cm (2½ inches) long; add to the pan.
5. At the end of cooking, there should be very little sauce. If there is too much left, remove the meat and vegetables and quickly reduce the sauce over a high flame before serving.

Tournedos with Cream Sauce (p30) ▶

Pièce de Boeuf aux Zestes d'Agrumes

Pot Roast with Citrus Peel

Serves 6. Preparation: 20 min
Cooking: 4 hr
★

- ○ **1.5kg (3¼ lb) top of rump, larded and bound by the butcher**
- ○ **1 lemon**
- ○ **1 orange**
- ○ **2 cloves garlic**
- ○ **3 onions**
- ○ **4 carrots**
- ○ **1 large potato**
- ○ **1 celery heart**
- ○ **250g (9 oz) ripe tomatoes**
- ○ **45ml (3 tbls) olive oil**
- ○ **5ml (1 tsp) rosemary**
- ○ **salt and pepper**

1. Wash the orange and lemon. From each cut a ribbon of peel, 2cm (¾ inch) by 6cm (2½ inches) without cutting into the pith. Refrigerate the fruit.
2. Peel the garlic and cut into fine slivers. Mix on a plate 5ml (1 tsp) each of salt and pepper and the crumbled rosemary. Roll the garlic slivers in this mixture, make incisions in the meat and insert the garlic.
3. Peel and finely chop the onions. Cut the celery into very thin slices. Wash and quarter the tomatoes and pass them through a vegetable mill. Peel the carrots and potato and chop into cubes 1cm (½ inch) square.
4. Preheat the oven to 170°C (325°F; gas mark 3). Heat the oil in an oval pan slightly deeper than the meat. Lightly brown the meat on all sides over a low heat for 10 minutes, then remove from the pan and add the onions and celery. Slightly brown these for 3 minutes, then replace the meat and add salt to taste.
5. Add the fruit peel, vegetables and tomato purée. Seal the pan with luting and cook for 3½ to 4 hours, or until tender.
6. When the meat is tender, remove it from the pan. Discard the fruit peel. Pass the sauce and vegetables through the vegetable mill. Add to this sauce the juice of ½ lemon and ½ orange, and salt and pepper to taste. Remove the string from the meat.

Serve the meat on a hot serving dish with the sauce in a sauceboat.

The tomato purée may be replaced by 200ml (7 fl oz) white wine.

Stews and casseroles from Provence always contain a piece of orange peel. Keep a stock of strips of dried orange peel which you have cut from fresh oranges.

When the piece of meat to be braised comes from the sirloin or the ribs it is 'marbled' and will certainly be tender, so it is unnecessary to lard it. Other cuts such as chuck are excellent but rather dry and may need to be larded before cooking in order to be sufficiently moist. The butcher can do this for you. It is also possible to buy a special utensil for larding. If you own one, try marinating for 2 hours, in a mixture of cognac, chopped parsley, garlic, nutmeg and spices, small sticks of fatty bacon which you then insert in your meat in the direction of the grain.

Estouffade aux Cèpes

Serves 6-7. Preparation: 25 min Cooking: 4 hr

Beef Stew with Dried Mushrooms

★ ★

○ **1.5kg (3¼ lb) beef (⅓ chuck,
  ⅓ flank, ⅓ silverside)**
○ **3 medium-sized onions**
○ **4 medium-sized carrots**
○ **600g (21 oz) ripe tomatoes**
○ **3 cloves garlic**
○ **1 bouquet garni consisting of:
  1 stick celery, 6 sprigs parsley,
  1 bay leaf, 1 sprig thyme**
○ **750ml (1 bottle) red wine (from
  Provence, if available)**
○ **100g (4 oz) dried mushrooms
  (cèpes)**
○ **45ml (3 tbls) olive oil**
○ **salt and pepper**

1. Put the mushrooms to soak in tepid water. Cut meat into cubes 3cm (1 inch) square and season them. Peel and finely mince the onions. Peel the carrots and slice into rounds. Leave the garlic cloves whole but pierce them with the point of a knife. Immerse the tomatoes in a saucepan of boiling water for 10 seconds, then peel them and cut them in half, remove their seeds and crush them roughly with a fork.

2. Heat the oil in a sauté pan large enough to hold all the cubes of meat in one layer. Place the meat in the pan with the onions and carrots. Cook for 10 minutes, without allowing them to brown, until there is no trace of pink in the meat and the onions are transparent. Pour the contents of the sauté pan into an earthenware or cast-iron stewpan, adding the tomatoes, garlic and bouquet garni. Mix together and pour in enough wine to barely cover the meat and vegetables.

3. Bring to the boil. Cover the pan and allow to simmer over a low heat for 3 hours.

4. After 3 hours of cooking add the drained and carefully washed mushrooms to the pan and continue to simmer until meat is tender (about 1 hour).

5. At the end of this time strain the contents of the pan through a sieve into a saucepan. Put the contents of the sieve back into the stewpan and cover. Reduce the sauce over a high flame for 5-10 minutes, until there is only enough sauce left to coat the meat. Season with salt and pepper to taste. Add to the meat and bring to the boil. Serve immediately.

Accompany this stew with macaroni or noodles with butter and grated cheese.

When reducing the sauce you can thicken it with 10ml (2 tsp) cornflour dissolved in 10ml (2 tsp) water.

The ideal cooking dish for braised meat, stews, etc, is a terrine – a traditional earthenware dish with a lid. It must be just big enough to hold all the ingredients: if you can avoid using too much liquid, you will obtain a richer sauce. The lid can be sealed with a paste of flour and water (luting paste) placed around the dish and its lid or by placing oiled greaseproof paper between the pan and its lid. The old-fashioned cast-iron dishes, which were left to cook on top of the stove for hours, had curved lids to house the contents, so that cooking was effected evenly all around the meat. Nowadays the oven performs this function.

Goulache

Goulash

○ **300g (10 oz) onions**
○ **50g (2 oz) lard**
○ **15ml (1 tbls) vinegar**
○ **10ml (2 tsp) paprika**
○ **800g (1¾ lb) neck of beef**
○ **300g (10 oz) tomatoes**
○ **1 clove garlic**
○ **marjoram**
○ **1 bay leaf**
○ **cumin**
○ **salt and pepper**

1. Chop the onions and brown in the lard in a stewpan. Baste them with the vinegar and sprinkle with paprika.
2. Add the meat, cut into large chunks the size of walnuts, stir and continue cooking.
3. Chop the tomatoes and add, together with the garlic, bay leaf and marjoram and cumin to taste. After about 30 minutes, season with salt and pepper. Continue cooking over a low heat until the meat is well cooked (about 1½ hours). The sauce should be thick but plentiful: if necessary add a little hot water while cooking.

Serve with boiled potatoes.

Daube aux Noix

Beef Stew with Walnuts

○ **800g (1¾ lb) neck of beef**
○ **200g (7 oz) onions**
○ **1 clove garlic**
○ **15ml (1 tbls) chopped parsley**
○ **1 bay leaf**
○ **2 cloves**
○ **salt and pepper**
○ **75ml (2½ fl oz) oil**
○ **75ml (2½ fl oz) vinegar**
○ **2.5ml (½ tsp) sugar**
○ **1 strip orange peel**
○ **12-16 walnut halves**

1. Cut the meat into large chunks, and place in an enamel or earthenware stewpan, together with the parsley, bay leaf, cloves, salt and pepper. Finely chop the garlic and onions and add to the meat.
2. Mix together the oil and vinegar and pour over the meat. Stir well, then cover and leave to marinate for 12 hours.
3. Preheat the oven to 160°C (300°F; gas mark 2). Add the sugar, orange peel and walnuts to the meat and its marinade, and stir well. Seal the pan with luting paste. Place in the preheated oven and cook for 1 hour at 160°C, then lower the heat to 120°C (250°F; gas mark ½) and cook 2 hours longer. When the meat is tender, remove the pan from the oven and, with a spoon, skim off any fat which has risen to the surface. Serve immediately from the cooking pot.

To skim off fat from a bouillon, let it stand for 15 minutes or more after removing from the heat. Then skim the top with a spoon. To degrease completely, pour the bouillon through a sieve lined with fine dampened white muslin which will hold all the fat. If you have the time, place the bouillon in the refrigerator. The fat will solidify on the surface and can easily be lifted off.

Beef Milan Style (p48) ▶

Daube aux Oeufs

Beef with Golden Eggs

Serves 4. Preparation and cooking: 3 hr

★★★

- ○ **250g (9 oz) onions**
- ○ **2 cloves garlic**
- ○ **bunch of mint**
- ○ **bunch of parsley**
- ○ **60ml (4 tbls) oil**
- ○ **salt**
- ○ **2.5ml (½ tsp) saffron**
- ○ **10ml (2 tsp) powdered ginger**
- ○ **800g (1¾ lb) neck of beef**
- ○ **4 eggs**

1. Peel and finely chop the onion. Peel and crush the garlic. Cut the meat into large chunks.
2. Tie the mint and parsley together.
3. Put the oil into a stewpan, add the garlic, salt, half the saffron, the ginger and 150ml (5 fl oz) water. Beat together with a fork until it becomes creamy. Add the meat and stir, then add the onion and mix all together.
4. Baste with 300ml (10 fl oz) water. Add the bunch of herbs and cover. Place the dish over a high flame until it boils, then lower the heat as much as possible and cook for two hours. The meat will be extremely tender. Remove the meat and the bunch of herbs from the dish. Put the meat in a warm place; discard the herbs.
5. Reduce the remaining juices to a syrupy sauce. This will take about 10 minutes. Meanwhile hard boil the eggs, then remove them from the water and shell them. In another saucepan, boil 480ml (18 fl oz) water with the remaining saffron. Plunge the eggs into this for 2 minutes: they will become yellow. Drain them and cut in half.
6. Now place the meat on a heated serving dish, cover with its sauce and garnish with the eggs. Serve immediately.

Boeuf à la Milanaise

Beef Milan Style

Serves 4. Preparation and cooking: 4 hr 30 min

- ○ **1kg (2¼ lb) chuck**
- ○ **50g (2 oz) ham**
- ○ **100g (4 oz) butter**
- ○ **300ml (10 fl oz) full-bodied red wine**
- ○ **1 pinch of mixed spice**
- ○ **2 cloves**
- ○ **2 mushroom broth cubes**
- ○ **nutmeg**
- ○ **salt and pepper**
- ○ **1 onion**
- ○ **1 carrot**
- ○ **1 stick celery**
- ○ **1 leek**
- ○ **2 cloves garlic**
- ○ **bunch of aromatic herbs: marjoram, sage, rosemary and basil**
- ○ **4 ripe tomatoes**

1. Chop finely together the vegetables, garlic and herbs. Lard the meat with the ham which has been cut into small strips, then brown in melted butter in a stewpan.
2. When it is well coloured, sprinkle with the wine and cover with the chopped vegetables. Add the mixed spice and the cloves and, gradually, the mushroom broth cubes dissolved in 480ml (18 fl oz) water. Flavour with a little grated nutmeg, salt and pepper. Cook, covered, over a low heat.
3. After 4 hours (or 1½ hours in a pressure cooker), the dish is ready. There should be sufficient gravy – add a little water during cooking if necessary.

This stew is even better reheated.

Boeuf à la Californie

Beef California Style

Serves 4. Preparation and cooking: 3 hr 30 min

★

- ○ 1 onion
- ○ 100g (4 oz) butter
- ○ 800g (1¾ lb) rump steak, not too lean
- ○ 150ml (5 fl oz) vinegar
- ○ 150ml (5 fl oz) cream
- ○ 75ml (2½ fl oz) beef stock (may be made from a cube)
- ○ salt and pepper

1. Chop the onion, heat the butter in a stewpan, add the onion and then the beef and brown lightly.
2. Gradually add the vinegar and, when absorbed, add 75ml (2½ fl oz) cream, a little at a time. When the cream has evaporated, slowly add the stock and season with salt and pepper.
3. Cook, covered, over a very low heat for 3 hours (or 45 minutes in a pressure cooker).
4. When the meat is tender, remove it from the pan, slice it and keep warm. Press the remaining cooking juices through a sieve and mix with the remaining cream. Heat the sauce, pour over the sliced meat and serve.

Daube de Boeuf

Beef in Red Wine

Serves 4. Preparation and cooking: 3 hr 15 min
Marinade: 24 hr

★ ★

- ○ 800g (1¾ lb) rump steak
- ○ 750ml (1 bottle) full-bodied red wine
- ○ 2 carrots
- ○ 2 onions
- ○ 1 handful mixed herbs, chopped
- ○ 150ml (5 fl oz) brandy
- ○ salt and pepper
- ○ nutmeg, cinnamon, curry powder (optional)

1. Cut the meat into chunks and place in a large bowl. Peel and chop the carrots and onions. Cover the meat with the wine and add the chopped vegetables and herbs, the brandy, salt, pepper and spices to taste. Leave to marinate, covered, in a cool place for 24 hours, then transfer everything to a stewpan and cook for 3 hours (or 45 minutes in a pressure cooker).
2. When the meat is tender, remove it from the sauce, place on a warmed serving dish and keep warm while you sieve the sauce. Pour over the sauce and serve immediately.

A boiled beef dish such as pot-au-feu *is a typical French one-course meal, but that doesn't mean that the usual problems surrounding any menu don't also apply here: what to serve before, with and after. What to serve before is simple: serve the bouillon, having carefully skimmed off the fat, in soup bowls or deep plates. Serve with toast and grated cheese and, possibly, a red wine from Bordeaux. Some, no doubt, will* faire chabrot, *that is, pour a little of their wine into their soup. If the* pot-au-feu *does not contain much meat, you can poach eggs in the soup and add a dash of port or a little cream. For the next course, to accompany the meat and vegetables, always have coarse sea salt, freshly milled pepper and plenty of pickles and sauces on hand: gherkins, small pickled onions, cherries or other fruits in vinegar, horseradish sauce, sweet and sour tomato relish, sauces of capers, shallots, mustard, herbs, anchovies, etc. Afterwards, serve some cheese. If you want to serve dessert as well, make sure it's very light.*

Boeuf à la Mode
Beef in Wine Marinade

Serves 6. Preparation and cooking: 3 hr 15 min Marinade: 12 hr

- ○ **1kg (2¼ lb) rump steak**
- ○ **100g (4 oz) butter**
- ○ **50g (2 oz) bacon**
- ○ **75ml (2½ fl oz) brandy**
- ○ **1 calf's foot**
- ○ **1 tomato**
- ○ **1 small leek**
- ○ **beef stock**
- ○ **300g (10 oz) small onions**
- ○ **300g (10 oz) new carrots**
- ○ **5ml (1 tsp) flour**
- ○ **salt and pepper**

For the marinade:
- ○ **450ml (15 fl oz) red wine**
- ○ **1 onion**
- ○ **1 carrot, cut into rounds**
- ○ **1 clove garlic**
- ○ **2 bay leaves**
- ○ **sprig parsley**
- ○ **150ml (5 fl oz) water**

1. Bind the meat so that it will keep its shape. Sprinkle with salt and pepper and place in a bowl. Mix all the ingredients for the marinade and leave the meat in this for 12 hours, turning from time to time.
2. After 12 hours, heat 50g (2 oz) butter in a stewpan and add the chopped bacon. Remove the meat from the marinade and brown it on all sides. Then sprinkle with the brandy and set alight. Let the flames die out.
3. Immerse the tomato in boiling water for 10 seconds, then peel.
4. Add to the meat the calf's foot, halved tomato, bay leaf, chopped leek, 200ml (7 fl oz) hot beef stock, 150ml (5 fl oz) strained marinade, and salt to taste. Cover the pan and cook over a very low heat for about 2 hours, adding a little strained marinade if necessary.
5. In a saucepan, melt the remaining butter, add the new carrots and small onions and salt to taste. Cook over a low heat for 30 minutes, basting with a little stock.
6. Remove the meat from the stewpan and keep warm. Sieve the contents left in the pan and add the flour mixed with a little stock. Cook the sauce until it thickens slightly, then pour some over the carrots and onions to glaze them.
7. Slice the meat, having removed the binding thread. Surround with the vegetables and pour the sauce over. Serve immediately.

Daube de Boeuf aux Haricots
Beef Stew with Haricot Beans

Serves 4. Preparation and cooking 2 hr 15 min

- ○ **300g (10 oz) haricot beans**
- ○ **300g (10 oz) chuck**
- ○ **100g (4 oz) smoked ham**
- ○ **300g (10 oz) gherkins**
- ○ **75ml (2½ fl oz) oil**
- ○ **20g (¾ oz) capers**
- ○ **150g (5 oz) pearl barley**
- ○ **salt and pepper**

1. Soak the beans and barley separately for 12 hours or overnight, then drain and rinse them. Reserve the barley. Bring to the boil 2 litres (3½ pints) water in a large pan, add the beans, lower the heat and simmer, partially covered, for about 1 hour, or until the beans are almost tender.
2. Cut the beef into small chunks, then, when the beans are tender, add the beef and cook for another hour.
3. Lightly brown the ham in a sauté pan, then add the gherkins, capers and oil. Mix well. Then add to the beans and beef, along with the barley. Continue cooking until the beef, beans and barley are all tender. Season and serve immediately.

This is a very ancient dish from the Mediterranean region. You can substitute rice for the barley – in this case you don't need to soak it, of course, and you would add it about 20 minutes before the meat and beans are ready.

Daube aux Petits Pois

Beef Stew with Peas

Serves 4. Preparation and cooking: 1 hr 45 min

★★

○ **800g (1¾ lb) rump steak, in one piece**
○ **200g (8 oz) cooked ham, in one slice**
○ **300g (10 oz) fresh peas (petits pois, if available)**
○ **1 onion**
○ **2 cloves**
○ **150ml (5 fl oz) dry white wine**
○ **150ml (5 fl oz) mushroom broth (made with stock cubes)**
○ **1 pinch curry powder**
○ **salt and pepper**

1. Place the beef in a stewpan. Cube the ham, shell the peas and add to the beef. Spike the onion with the cloves and add. Pour over the wine.
2. Cook over a medium heat for 1½ hours, turning the meat every now and then, and basting with the stock.
3. Add the curry powder and season with salt and pepper. Place on a hot serving dish, slice and serve very hot. This dish is best when eaten the day after it is prepared.

Boeuf à la Moelle

Shin of Beef Peasant Style

Serves 4. Preparation and cooking: 2 hr

★★

○ **4 pieces of shin on the bone, 200g (7 oz) each**
○ **flour**
○ **1 onion**
○ **1 clove garlic**
○ **1 carrot**
○ **1 stick celery**
○ **50g (2 oz) bacon**
○ **40g (1¾ oz) butter**
○ **45ml (3 tbls) oil**
○ **salt and pepper**
○ **150ml (5 fl oz) dry white wine**
○ **150ml (5 fl oz) beef stock**
○ **45ml (3 tbls) tomato purée**
○ **250g (9 oz) petits pois**

1. Place some flour on a plate and dip the pieces of meat into it, then tie them up so that they don't lose their shape during cooking.
2. Finely chop the onion, garlic, carrot, celery and bacon. Heat the oil and butter in a stewpan, add the chopped mixture and fry lightly. Add the beef and brown on all sides. Add the wine and salt and pepper to taste.
3. When the wine has completely evaporated, add the hot stock mixed with the tomato purée. Turn the heat down very low and allow the meat to cook, covered, for about 1 hour 20 minutes, turning often and basting with the sauce.
4. Three-quarters of the way through cooking, add the peas which have been drained and rinsed. When cooked, place the meat with its sauce on a hot serving dish and serve immediately.

Boeuf en Cocotte aux Oignons

Beef Stew with Onions

*Serves 4. Preparation: 20 min
Cooking: 5 hr 10 min*

★

○ **1kg (2¼ lb) rump or flank, larded and bound by the butcher**
○ **1kg (2¼ lb) large onions**
○ **7 cloves**
○ **400g (14 oz) medium spaghetti**
○ **50g (2 oz) grated Parmesan cheese**
○ **salt and pepper**

1. Preheat the oven to 120°C (250°F; gas mark ½). Peel the onions and cut them into rounds 1cm (½ inch) thick. Cover the base of an earthenware dish with them and add salt. Spike the meat with the cloves, add salt and pepper and place on the bed of onions. Cover and cook in the oven for 5 hours. Turn the meat over once or twice during this time.
2. Remove the meat from the pot and arrange on a hot serving dish. Remove the string. Decorate with half the onions separated into rings (they will have remained whole despite their long cooking). Cover the dish with aluminium foil and keep warm in the turned-off oven.
3. Bring some water to the boil in a large saucepan, add salt and then the spaghetti. Pass the rest of the onions and the remaining cooking juices through a vegetable mill into a saucepan. When the spaghetti is just tender (*al dente*), drain it and add to the saucepan. Cook on a very low heat for 1 minute, stirring, then pour into a hot serving dish. Serve the spaghetti together with the meat, which you slice at table. Serve with grated Parmesan cheese and freshly ground black pepper.

Broufado

Serves 6-7. Preparation: 15 min Cooking: 4 hr 15 min Marinade: 24 hr

Beef Stew Provence Style

○ **1.5kg (3¼ lb) flank**
○ **2 medium-sized onions**
○ **½ litre (18 fl oz) white wine**
○ **60ml (4 tbls) vinegar**
○ **50ml (1¾ fl oz) cognac**
○ **1 sprig thyme**
○ **1 bay leaf**
○ **4 sprigs parsley**
○ **1 clove garlic**
○ **4 gherkins, cut into rounds**
○ **45ml (3 tbls) capers, drained**
○ **3 anchovies in salt**
○ **10ml (2 tsp) cornflour**
○ **90ml (6 tbls) olive oil**
○ **salt and pepper**

1. The day before: cut the meat into cubes 4cm (2 inches) square. Peel the onions and grate them over a bowl, add the vinegar, cognac and 60ml (4 tbls) oil. Beat with a fork, then add the meat, stir and refrigerate for 24 hours, turning the meat 2 or 3 times.
2. The following day: place the meat and its marinade in a terracotta or cast-iron stewpan. Salt lightly. Peel the garlic clove, crush and add to the meat. Bind together the thyme, bay leaf and parsley and add this, then pour in the wine. Cover, bring to the boil, then lower the heat and allow to simmer very slowly for 3 hours. Alternatively, bring to the boil on top of the stove, then put into a preheated oven set at 140°C (275°F; gas mark 1).
3. After 3 hours, add the capers and gherkins. Allow to simmer for another hour or more, until the meat is very tender.
4. When the meat is cooked, dissolve the cornflour in 30ml (2 tbls) cold water and add to the ingredients in the pan while stirring.
5. Wash the anchovies and separate them into fillets. Chop them into small pieces, add to the pan with the remaining oil and allow to simmer for 15 minutes. Remove the bouquet garni, taste the sauce and season. Serve hot.

Chili con Carne

Serves 6. Preparation: 20 min Cooking: 2 hr

Chili con Carne

★

○ **1.5kg (3¼ lb) beef: silverside or blade**
○ **4 medium-sized onions**
○ **2 cloves garlic**
○ **15-60ml (1-4 tbls) chili powder**
○ **5ml (1 tsp) oregano**
○ **2.5ml (½ tsp) cumin**
○ **45ml (3 tbls) oil**
○ **salt and pepper**

1. Cut the meat into tiny cubes of 1cm (½ inch) or smaller. Peel and chop the onions, peel and finely chop the garlic. Heat the oil in a sauté pan and lightly brown the pieces of meat over a high flame. Remove them with a skimmer and place in a stewpan.
2. Lightly brown the onions and garlic in the same oil, then add to the meat. Add the chili powder, oregano and cumin, and salt and pepper to taste. Barely cover with water (or with beef stock if you have some available) and allow to simmer for 2 hours or more, until the meat is tender. Serve immediately.

This Mexican dish is very highly spiced. You can cook dried red kidney beans separately (soak them overnight first, and be sure to cook them until they are soft) and add them to the chili con carne 15 minutes before it is done.

Estouffade aux Olives Vertes

Serves 6. Preparation: 25 min Cooking: 4 hr

Beef Stew with Green Olives

★ ★

○ **1.5kg (3¼ lb) beef: ½ flank, ½ chuck**
○ **750ml (1 bottle) dry white wine**
○ **4 large onions**
○ **250g (9 oz) lean, mild-cure bacon**
○ **250g (9 oz) button mushrooms**
○ **250g (9 oz) pitted green olives**
○ **1 sprig thyme**
○ **1 bay leaf**
○ **6 sprigs parsley**
○ **30ml (2 tbls) flour**
○ **30ml (2 tbls) oil**
○ **25g (1 oz) butter**
○ **salt and freshly ground black pepper**

1. Cut the meat into cubes 4cm (2 inches) square. Cut the bacon into sticks 1cm (½ inch) thick. Finely chop the onions.
2. Heat the oil in a stewpan, add the bacon and cook for 10 minutes over a low heat until the bacon fat is transparent and the meat is lightly browned, then remove with a skimmer and reserve.
3. Add several pieces of meat to the stewpan and brown lightly for about 5 minutes, then remove them from the pan and put aside. Repeat until all the meat has been browned. (You do not want the pieces of meat to touch each other: if the pan is too crowded, the meat will not be properly sealed.)
4. Discard most of the fat from the pan, add the onions and cook them until they are transparent but not brown, then sprinkle them with flour, turning with a spatula. As soon as the flour starts to brown, add the wine slowly, stirring constantly.
5. Bring to the boil. Tie together with white thread the bay leaf, thyme and parsley. Add this bouquet garni to the onions, along with the beef and a pinch of salt. As soon as it starts to boil again cover the pan and leave to simmer over a low heat. The dish can also be put into a preheated oven at 140°C (275°F; gas mark 1).
6. After 3 hours, remove the pieces of beef and the bouquet garni from the pan and reserve them. Pass the cooking juices and bits of onion through the fine mesh of a vegetable mill and return this purée to the stewpan. Add the beef, bouquet garni and sticks of bacon.
7. Trim the earthy base from the mushrooms, wash and dry them, slice them thinly and add to the stewpan.
8. Bring to the boil 2 litres (3½ pints) water in a saucepan, blanch the olives for 5 minutes, then drain them and add to the stewpan. Cover and simmer for another 45 minutes or more, until the meat is tender and the sauce much reduced and velvety.
9. When the stew is ready remove the bouquet garni, taste and add salt if necessary, and pepper as desired, arrange on a hot serving dish and served immediately.

Accompany this delicate dish with small boiled potatoes.

Taste the olives you intend to add to a dish before you do so, as they are often very salty. If this is the case, pit them, rinse thoroughly and blanch them for 5 minutes in a large quantity of boiling water.

In olden times, beef stew was eaten with a spoon. Whether we care to do so today or not, the meat should still be tender enough so that a knife is not necessary to cut it. Therefore the beef we choose must be of prime quality and cooked very slowly for a long time. Meat cooked in this way is particularly delicious and juicy, since after the initial phase of cooking when the meat exudes its juices into the stew, it later reabsorbs the same juices mixed with the sauce. The result is a marvellous meat stew with a thick, tasty sauce and tender meat which melts in the mouth. If you intend to serve the stew hot, don't leave it uncovered, because it will dry out very quickly. Keep it covered and baste it or turn it over in the sauce to keep it moist.

Beef Stew with Haricot Beans (p50) ▶

Bouilli à la Bretonne

Serves 8. Preparation: 30 min Cooking: 4 hr 30 min

Boiled Beef Breton Style

★ ★ ★

- ○ **1.5kg (3¼ lb) chuck**
- ○ **3 carrots**
- ○ **3 turnips**
- ○ **1 stick celery**
- ○ **1 onion**
- ○ **2 cloves**
- ○ **thyme**
- ○ **1 bay leaf**
- ○ **10 coriander seeds**
- ○ **5ml (1 tsp) peppercorns**
- ○ **5ml (1 tsp) coarse salt**
- ○ **250g (9 oz) buckwheat flour**
- ○ **100g (4 oz) butter**
- ○ **75ml (2½ fl oz) milk**
- ○ **1 egg**
- ○ **120ml (4 fl oz) cream**
- ○ **15ml (1 tbls) sugar**
- ○ **100g (4 oz) raisins**
- ○ **1 small savoy cabage**
- ○ **salt and pepper**

1. Bring to the boil 3 litres (5¼ pints) water in a large saucepan. Add the meat and return to the boil. Then lower the heat and cook for 30 minutes, skimming often. In a small bowl, soak the raisins in hot water to cover.
2. Meanwhile, clean the carrots, turnips and celery. At the end of 30 minutes, add them to the beef, along with the onion spiked with cloves, thyme, bay leaf, coriander, peppercorns and coarse salt. Put the flour into a bowl. Take 1 ladleful of the broth and mix it with 60g (2¼ oz) butter. Add this mixture to the flour. Mix well and add milk, cream, egg and sugar, stirring continuously. Add the drained raisins and mix again.
3. Enclose this mixture in a white cloth, forming a roll. Make a knot at each end. Cook the meat for a further 2½ hours, then plunge the roll into the soup and cook for 1½ hours.
4. Meanwhile, prepare the cabbage. Cut into 4 and boil for 5 minutes in salted water, then drain.
5. Melt the remaining butter in a pot, add the cabbage and salt and pepper to taste and cook, covered, over a low heat (adding a little soup if necessary) until it is tender. At this time the mixture in the cloth roll should be cooked, so remove it from the soup.
6. Remove the meat from the soup and slice. Arrange the meat on a warmed serving dish. Unroll the cloth and crumble its contents around the meat. Complete the dish with the well-drained vegetables from the soup and the cabbage. Pour the soup into a tureen and serve separately; it will provide a sauce.

It is always best to prepare a stew with the same wine you intend to serve with the meal.

Daubes *are very delicious, and very popular in France. This method of cooking meat is very ancient and still deserves to be appreciated today. It involves cooking in a covered pot, as slowly and for as long as possible, meat which may or may not have been marinated. The marinade would usually consist of red or white wine, sometimes seasoned with vinegar, with a bouquet garni, spices and chopped or sliced vegetables. Sometimes the meat is sealed in hot oil before it is placed in its marinade. All* daubes *are better when reheated and all can be eaten cold with salads and garlic* croûtons. *If you prefer a jellied* daube, *add 1 or 2 calf's feet (preferably blanched) when you cook it.*

Boeuf à la Ficelle
Boiled Beef on a String

Serves 4. Preparation: 15 min Cooking: 40 min

★ ★

○ **800g (1¾ lb) fillet or rump,
  bound but not barded**
○ **8 new carrots, peeled**
○ **8 small leeks, peeled**
○ **8 small turnips, peeled**
○ **2 celery hearts, quartered**
○ **4 small onions**
○ **4 sprigs chervil**
○ **2 sprigs parsley**
○ **1 sprig tarragon**
○ **2 cloves**
○ **12 peppercorns**
○ **15ml (1 tbls) sea salt**

1. Bring to the boil 2.5 litres (4½ pints) water in a large saucepan, add salt, peppercorns and cloves and then the prepared vegetables. Tie together the parsley, chervil and tarragon to make a bouquet garni. Add to the water and simmer for 10 minutes.
2. Meanwhile, tie a string at each end of the piece of beef, long enough to be able to tie to the handles of the saucepan so you can remove the meat easily.
3. When the vegetables have cooked for 15 minutes, plunge the meat into the pan, keeping it barely immersed, and tie the string to the handles of the pan. Allow it to cook for 25 minutes at a gentle boil for medium beef, pink at the centre. Skim as necessary.
4. When the meat is cooked, remove it from the pan by the strings and place it on a board. Remove the strings and cut the meat into 4 thick slices. Arrange on a hot serving dish. Remove the vegetables with the skimmer, garnish the meat with them and serve immediately. Accompany with mustard, coarse sea salt and gherkins, with *sauce verte* (mayonnaise, to which a purée of green herbs has been added) or cold tomato sauce with capers.

The meat can also be sliced before cooking for 10 to 15 minutes. You can serve the cooking liquid as a soup if, instead of using water for cooking, you use beef stock.

Pot-au-Feu à la Provencale
Boiled Beef Provence Style

Serves 8. Preparation and cooking: 4 hr

★ ★

○ **800g (1¾ lb) silverside**
○ **500g (18 oz) topside on the
  bone**
○ **500g (18 oz) shoulder of beef**
○ **600g (21 oz) shoulder of lamb**
○ **600g (21 oz) leg of veal**
○ **200g (7 oz) lean bacon**
○ **1 onion spiked with 3 cloves**
○ **3 turnips**
○ **8 leeks**
○ **8 carrots**
○ **2 tomatoes**
○ **3 cloves garlic**
○ **1 sprig thyme**
○ **1 bay leaf**
○ **2 celery sticks**
○ **6 juniper berries**
○ **6 black peppercorns**
○ **200ml (7 fl oz) dry white wine**
○ **salt**

1. Pour 4 litres (7 pints) cold water into a large saucepan and add the topside on the bone and shoulder of beef. Bring to the boil slowly, over a low heat. Skim, then add the silverside, lamb, veal and bacon. Bring back to the boil and skim carefully, then add salt and wine. Tie together the thyme, bay leaf and celery and add this bouquet garni to the pan along with the spiked onion, unpeeled garlic, juniper berries and peppercorns.
2. When the water boils, lower the heat so that it simmers gently for 1½ hours.
3. At the end of this time, peel and wash the turnips, carrots and leeks. Remove most of the green of the leeks and tie together the white parts. Plunge these vegetables into the pan along with the unpeeled, washed tomatoes. Continue to cook for 1½ to 2 hours, until all the meat is tender.
4. When the *pot-au-feu* is ready, sieve the liquid, skim off the fat and serve in a soup bowl. Put the meats – except the topside and the shoulder, which will be served after the other meats – on a hot serving dish. Surround with the vegetables and serve immediately.

Traditionally, this is served with a salad of chickpeas dressed with wine vinegar and olive oil, capers, gherkins and black olives and served lukewarm, and with a tomato sauce. Or you could cook some thin spaghetti in the stock to accompany the meat and vegetables.

Queue en Hochepot

Serves 6. Preparation: 10 min Cooking: 4 hr

Oxtail Hot Pot

★★

○ **1 oxtail in 4cm (1½ inch) segments**
○ **2 pig trotters**
○ **1 pig's ear**
○ **1 small cabbage**
○ **6 carrots**
○ **6 turnips**
○ **salt**

1. Place the oxtail, trotters and pig's ear in a large pan. Cover with water and bring to the boil over a moderate heat, removing the scum as it appears. Once it has boiled, lower the heat and leave to simmer for 2 hours.
2. Peel the vegetables; quarter the cabbage, removing the hard centre. Leave them to stand in a basin of cold water.
3. After 2 hours, salt the stockpot and add the vegetables to it. If there is not enough liquid, add some hot water but make sure you do not cover the vegetables. Bring back to the boil on a higher heat, then lower again and simmer for a further 2 hours until the meat and vegetables are tender.
4. When all is ready remove from the heat. Slice the ear thinly, bone the trotters and cut into small pieces. Arrange the meat and vegetables on a serving dish. The stock can be kept to be used for another dish, or it can be poured into a gravyboat and served, but be sure you skim off the fat first.

Accompany this springtime dish with new potatoes and grilled chipolata sausages.

Pot-au-Feu à la Flamande

Serves 4-6. Preparation and cooking: 4 hr

Flemish Hot Pot

★★

○ **1.5kg (3¼ lb) flank or brisket, in one piece**
○ **1kg (2¼ lb) carrots**
○ **1kg (2¼ lb) floury potatoes**
○ **4 medium onions**
○ **salt and pepper**

1. Bring 2 litres (72 fl oz) of water to the boil in a large pan, place the piece of beef in it and wait until it boils again. Remove the scum, then add salt, lower the heat and simmer for 1 hour.
2. Now peel the onions, chop them into rough pieces and add to the pan. Peel the carrots, slice across in thick chunks and leave to stand in a basin of cold water. Peel and quarter the potatoes and do the same. After the onions have cooked for an hour drain the carrots and add to the pan. Continue cooking over a low heat. One hour later add the potatoes and cook for another hour. By then the meat should be tender and the stock almost entirely have evaporated. If not, cook for a little longer.
3. When everything is ready, remove the meat from the pot and slice finely, removing the bone and the fatty pieces. Arrange on a serving dish and cover with an aluminium lid to keep hot. If there is some stock left reduce it over a high heat, stirring the vegetables to prevent them from sticking, then mash them with a fork. Season if necessary. Surround the meat with the mashed vegetables and serve.

Shin of Beef Peasant Style (p52) ▶

Langue de Boeuf Gros Sel

Serves 4-6. Preparation and cooking: 2 hr 30 min

Boiled Tongue with Vegetables

★★

○ 1 trimmed beef tongue
○ 6 carrots
○ 6 turnips
○ 6 leeks
○ 6 potatoes
○ 1 onion spiked with 1 clove
○ 3 sprigs parsley
○ 1 small stick celery
○ 1 small sprig thyme
○ ½ bay leaf
○ coarse salt
○ table salt

1. Wash the tongue very carefully, then place in a pan, cover generously with cold water and bring to the boil over a medium heat. Then lower the heat and allow to simmer gently, skimming the froth as it appears, for 30 minutes.
2. At the end of this time, remove the tongue from the pan and drain well. Allow the meat to cool a little, then peel and return to the washed pan, cover with 2½ litres (4½ pints) cold water and bring to the boil. Tie together the parsley, celery, thyme and bay leaf and add this bouquet garni to the pan, along with the spiked onion. Add 10ml (2 tsp) coarse salt and allow to boil gently for 2 hours, partially covered.
3. At the end of 1 hour, peel the carrots, leeks and turnips and add them to the pan. Peel the potatoes and place in a small saucepan. Cover with cold water, add salt and cook on a low heat. When the potatoes are tender turn off the heat and cover to keep warm.
4. After the vegetables have cooked for 45 minutes, they and the tongue should be tender. Remove the tongue from the pan, cut into slices ½cm (¼ inch) thick and arrange on a hot serving dish. Surround the meat with the vegetables and the drained potatoes. Baste everything with a little bouillon. Serve the bouillon separately as soup, accompanied by coarse sea salt, gherkins, various kinds of mustards and small pickled onions.

You can serve the soup with croûtons (slices of bread cut into triangles or other shapes and sautéed in butter) and grated cheese, and the tongue with a tomato or spicy onion sauce.

Flanchet Farci au Vert

Serves 6. Preparation: 30 min Cooking: 3 hr 30 min

Stuffed Beef Flank

★★★

○ 1.5kg (3¼ lb) flank
○ 250g (9 oz) minced silverside
○ 150g (5 oz) chard leaves
○ 150g (5 oz) spinach
○ 15ml (1 tbls) chopped parsley
○ 100g (4 oz) grated Gruyère cheese
○ 1 egg
○ 50g (2 oz) white bread, crusts removed
○ 100ml (3½ fl oz) milk
○ 6 carrots
○ 3 turnips
○ 6 small leeks
○ 1 head celery
○ 1 onion spiked with 3 cloves
○ 1 sprig thyme
○ 1 bay leaf
○ 4 sprigs parsley
○ nutmeg
○ salt and pepper

1. Ask your butcher to make a slit in the meat, forming a pocket. Wash the spinach and remove the stalks. Wash the chard. (If chard is not available, use double the amount of spinach.) Place the spinach and the chard, with the water still clinging to their leaves, in a large saucepan. Salt lightly, cover and cook over a high flame for 4 minutes. Then drain thoroughly, pressing to extract all the water, and chop finely. Place in a bowl with the minced silverside, chopped parsley, grated cheese, egg and salt, pepper and nutmeg to taste.
2. Heat the milk in a small saucepan, add the bread which you have broken up, boil for 1 minute and add to the salad bowl. Mix well.
3. Stuff the meat with this mixture and sew up the opening with coarse white thread. Cut off the celery leaves and tie them together with the thyme, bay leaf and parsley to form a bouquet garni.
4. In a large pan, place the meat, spiked onion and bouquet garni. Cover generously with cold water and place over a medium heat. When it boils, skim, add salt, lower the heat and allow to simmer gently for 3½ hours.
5. 1 hour before the end of cooking, add the peeled vegetables.
6. When meat and vegetables are tender, remove from the pan and arrange on a hot serving dish. Slice the meat and keep warm. Remove and discard the onion and bouquet garni, pass the stock through a fine strainer, pour into a soup bowl and serve very hot.

Marmite Milanaise en Sauce Verte

Milanese Stew with Green Sauce

Serves 12.
Preparation and cooking: 4 hr 30 min
★ ★

○ **1kg (2¼ lb) rump, larded and bound by the butcher**
○ **1kg (2¼ lb) rib of beef, bound**
○ **1 ox tongue, trimmed**
○ **800g (1¾ lb) shin of veal, boned and bound**
○ **1 small chicken**
○ **500g (18 oz) Italian spiced sausage (cotechino) or Lyons sausage**
○ **salt**

For the green sauce:
○ **2 small onions**
○ **1 clove garlic**
○ **6 anchovies in salt**
○ **45ml (3 tbls) capers**
○ **60ml (4 tbls) chopped parsley**
○ **30ml (2 tbls) lemon juice**
○ **30ml (2 tbls) vinegar**
○ **150ml (5 fl oz) olive oil**
○ **pepper**

1. Place the rib in a large saucepan, cover generously with cold water and bring to the boil over a low heat, skimming as necessary. When boiling point is reached, add salt and the bound piece of rump. Leave to cook for 1½ hours before adding the chicken.
2. Meanwhile, blanch the tongue in boiling water for 10 minutes.
3. 30 minutes after the chicken is added, add the veal and tongue. To recap: 4½ hours for the rib, 4 hours for the rump, 2½ hours for the chicken and 2 hours for the tongue and the veal. Skim every time meat is added to the pot. If necessary, add more boiling water, but only in small quantities, because the bouillon must be very reduced and only barely cover the meat. Traditionally, not even aromatic herbs are added to the bouillon – this is an all-meat stew. You might add 1 carrot, 1 onion, 1 stick celery and a tiny bouquet garni, but nothing else.
4. 1 hour before the end of cooking, pierce the sausage with a fork and place in a saucepan of cold water. Boil gently for 1 hour. When cooked, add the sausage to the other meats, which will also be cooked by then.
5. Meanwhile, prepare the green sauce: peel the onions and cloves of garlic and chop finely. Wash the anchovies, separate into fillets and chop into small pieces, likewise the capers. Put these ingredients into a bowl with the parsley, add vinegar, lemon juice and pepper and incorporate the oil very slowly by beating with a fork, as if making a mayonnaise. Refrigerate until you are ready to serve it.
6. When everything is ready, peel the tongue and slice thinly. Cut up the chicken. Arrange all the different types of meat on a hot serving dish, baste with bouillon and serve. Serve the green sauce separately, and some of the bouillon in a soup bowl.

This dish may be served with spinach or mashed potatoes, as they do in the Piedmont region of northern Italy, where they also serve fruits pickled in vinegar, known as *mostarda.*

Don't cook cabbage with boiled beef without having blanched it first, as its flavour will dominate everything. In addition, a stock in which cabbage was boiled will not last as long as one cooked without it. For best results, cook the cabbage separately in some of the stock with, perhaps, a piece of bacon.

Boiled beef should cook uncovered: its delicious smell will spread through the whole house, creating a warm, cosy atmosphere. If you want to have good soup*, put the meat into cold water; if you want the* meat *to be especially savoury, then put it into boiling water. Meat plunged into cold water gives all its juices and flavour to the soup; in boiling water it is immediately sealed. If you want both good stock and savoury meat, plunge the first type of meat (for instance the ribs) into cold water, then when the water boils add the rest of the meat. Save the former for the next day to mince or to make a salad with; the second lot of meat is best served very hot with the vegetables it was cooked with.*

Soupe Lombarde
Soup Lombardy Style

Serves 4. Preparation and cooking: 1 hr 15 min

★★

○ **1 small savoy cabbage**
○ **400g (14 oz) flank**
○ **1 clove garlic**
○ **1 onion**
○ **1 stick celery**
○ **1 beef stock cube**
○ **150g (5 oz) rice**
○ **handful parsley**
○ **freshly grated Parmesan cheese**
○ **salt and pepper**

1. Trim the cabbage and remove the outer leaves. Wash and cut up. Cut the flank into chunks. Chop the garlic and onion. Cut the celery into chunks.
2. Put everything into a stewpan with 1½ litres (2¾ pints) water and the stock cube and bring to a boil, then lower the heat and simmer for about 40 minutes. Then add the rice and parsley and continue cooking until the rice is tender. Add the grated Parmesan.
3. Allow the soup to stand for a few minutes, then serve very hot. This is an ideal winter soup.

Anneaux de Courgettes à la Coriandre
Courgette Rings with Coriander

Serves 4-5.
Preparation and cooking: 1 hr

★

○ **400g (14 oz) steak minced with 50g (2 oz) beef kidney fat**
○ **5 medium-sized courgettes: approx 1.2kg (2½ lb)**
○ **30ml (2 tbls) chopped fresh coriander**
○ **15ml (1 tbls) chopped parsley**
○ **3 medium-sized onions**
○ **50g (2 oz) butter**
○ **1 pinch cayenne pepper**
○ **salt and pepper**

1. Ask your butcher to mince together the beef and the kidney fat.
2. Put the meat in a bowl, add salt, pepper generously, and add 15ml (1 tbls) chopped coriander and the parsley. Mix well with your fingertips.
3. Peel the onions and grate them finely. Add one-third to the mince and mix again.
4. Place the remainder of the onions in a large saucepan 25cm (10 inches) across and add the butter and ½ litre (18 fl oz) water, the cayenne and salt and pepper to taste. Bring to the boil, cover and leave to cook over a low heat for 15 minutes.
5. Meanwhile, prepare the courgette rings: wash the courgettes, wipe them dry, cut off the ends and cut into slices 2.5cm (1 inch) thick. Depending on the size of the courgettes, you should obtain about 25 rounds. With a small spoon, scoop out the seeds so that only the pulp and the skin remain.
6. Fill the rings with the beef mixture. When the onions have cooked for 15 minutes, add the stuffed courgettes and salt. Cover and cook for 15 minutes on a low heat.
7. Turn the rings and cook, covered, for a further 15 minutes then remove the lid, increase the heat and cook for 8-10 minutes, until the sauce has reduced to one-third of its original volume and has a syrupy consistency.
8. Turn the rings once during the reduction of the sauce, then remove them from the pan with a skimmer, and arrange on a hot serving dish.
9. Add the remaining coriander to the sauce, stir well and pour over the courgette rings. Serve immediately.

Steak Tartare

Steak Tartare

Serves 4. Preparation: 20 min

★ ★

○ **500g (18 oz) fillet**
○ **salt and pepper**
○ **mustard**
○ **75ml (2½ fl oz) oil**
○ **juice of 1 lemon**
○ **few drops Tabasco sauce**
○ **2 dashes Worcestershire sauce**
○ **4 eggs**
○ **2 onions**
○ **few sprigs parsley**
○ **large handful capers**
○ **12 pickled gherkins**

1. Mince the fillet in a mincer (or better still, use a large knife). Place in a bowl and season with salt and pepper.
2. In another bowl, mix the mustard with the oil, then add lemon juice, Tabasco and Worcestershire sauce. Add to the minced meat, season well and divide the meat into 4 equal portions. Form into round patties and place on 4 plates.
3. Make a hollow in the centre of each patty and stand half an eggshell in it with 1 egg yolk in each. Finely chop the onions; chop the parsley. Leave the capers whole; slice the gherkins.
4. Surround each patty with small heaps of onion, parsley and capers, alternating with gherkins. Serve cool but not very cold. To eat, each person mixes the egg yolk into the meat, discarding the shell, and adds the other ingredients to taste.

Bifteck Haché à la Russe

Russian Hamburgers

Serves 4. Preparation and cooking: 20 min

★ ★

○ **400g (14 oz) minced flank**
○ **100g (4 oz) butter**
○ **salt and pepper**
○ **nutmeg**
○ **oil**
○ **75ml (2½ fl oz) yogurt**

1. Place the minced meat in a bowl and add 70g (3 oz) soft butter, cut into small pieces, and a pinch each of salt, pepper and grated nutmeg. Mix the ingredients carefully so that the butter mixes properly with the meat.
2. Make hamburgers with this mixture, coat them with oil and arrange under a very hot grill. Cook on both sides for 10 minutes then place on a hot serving dish.
3. Just before they are cooked, melt the remaining butter, mix with the yogurt and stir for a few seconds. Pour this sauce over the hamburgers and serve immediately.

Galettes aux Beurre

Beef Pancakes with Butter

Serves 4-5. Preparation: 15 min Cooking: 10 min

 ★

○ **600g (1 lb 5 oz) minced steak**
○ **200g (8 oz) soft butter**
○ **30ml (2 tbls) Madeira**
○ **1 egg**
○ **15ml (1 tbls) flour**
○ **30ml (2 tbls) white breadcrumbs**
○ **150g (6 oz) fresh cream**
○ **7.5ml (1½ tsp) oil**
○ **pinch nutmeg**
○ **salt and pepper**

1. Put the meat in a dish, moisten with 15ml (1 tbls) of Madeira, and season. Add a pinch of nutmeg, 150g (6 oz) of soft butter and blend all together well with a wooden spoon, two forks or – better still – your hands, until perfectly smooth.
2. Beat the egg well in a bowl with a little salt and pepper. Put the flour on one flat plate and the breadcrumbs on another.
3. Divide the mixture into 8 equal parts, roll them into balls between your hands, then flatten into thin cakes 1.5cm (½ inch) thick. Dip them in the flour, then the beaten egg, then the breadcrumbs, and leave on a board.
4. Heat the oil in a frying pan, add to it the remaining 50g (2 oz) of butter and fry the cakes over a low heat until they are golden brown, about 2 minutes each side. Remove with a spatula and arrange around a serving dish kept hot over a pan of boiling water.
5. Pour away the cooking fat, glaze the frying pan with the other 15ml (1 tbls) of Madeira. When it has evaporated add the fresh cream. Boil for 30 seconds and pour into the centre of the cakes in the dish, and serve.

Saucisses aux Quatre-Épices

Spiced Sausages

Serves 6. Preparation: 10 min Cooking: 10 min

★

- ○ **1kg (2¼ lb) flank minced with 100g (4 oz) beef kidney**
- ○ **2.5ml (½ tsp) mixed spice**
- ○ **3 pinches thyme**
- ○ **2 cloves garlic**
- ○ **100ml (3½ fl oz) beef stock**
- ○ **salt and freshly ground black pepper**

1. Place the minced meat in a bowl. Peel the garlic and put through a garlic press into the bowl. Add the mixed spice, thyme, salt and pepper to taste. Mix with your hands, then moisten with the stock and mix again until the stock is well absorbed. Divide the mixture into 18 equal parts and form into small sausages 9cm (3½ inches) long, moistening your hands in cold water while you do so.
2. Heat the grill or prepare a barbecue and cook the sausages until they are well browned, about 8-10 minutes.

In Romania, where these sausages (*mititei*) originate, they are served with grilled peppers or marinated cucumbers.

Bouchées aux Amandes

Almond Meatballs

Serves 3-4. Preparation: 20 min Cooking: 15 min

★

- ○ **400g (14 oz) minced steak**
- ○ **20 blanched almonds**
- ○ **20ml (4 tsp) very fine semolina**
- ○ **250g (9 oz) double cream**
- ○ **1 lemon**
- ○ **5ml (1 tsp) curry powder**
- ○ **30ml (2 tbls) flour**
- ○ **30ml (2 tbls) oil**
- ○ **50g (2 oz) butter**
- ○ **salt and pepper**

1. Place the meat in a bowl, season, add 45ml (3 tbls) cream and work mixture until it is well blended.
2. Wash and wipe dry the lemon, grate three-quarters of the rind (only the yellow part, not the white pith) on a fine grater over the dish containing the meat, add the semolina and work everything together well.
3. Put the flour on a plate. Divide the meat into 20 equal parts, dust your hands with flour and roll each portion of meat into a round ball. Place an almond in the centre of each, then roll again to close up.
4. Repeat until all the ingredients have been used up, then heat the oil in frying pan just large enough to hold all the meatballs in one layer. Add the butter and when it is melted add the meatballs.
5. Cook over a low heat for about 10 minutes until the meatballs are well browned. To turn them, shake the pan: the meatballs will roll about and cook uniformly.
6. When the meatballs are cooked, remove from pan with a skimmer, place on a hot dish and keep warm. Discard the cooking fat, squeeze the lemon over the pan, and, over a high flame, scrape the bottom to deglaze. Then add the cream, curry powder, salt and pepper. Boil for 3 minutes until the cream is reduced by half, put the meatballs back in the pan and roll them about in the sauce.
7. When the meatballs are well covered with the sauce, pour the contents of the pan onto a hot serving dish and serve immediately.

Accompany with a rice pilau.

Kefta au Coulis d'Oignons

Serves 4-5. Preparation and cooking: 1 hr

Meatballs with Spiced Onion Sauce

★

- ○ **500g (18 oz) steak minced with 50g (2 oz) beef kidney fat**
- ○ **500g (18 oz) onions**
- ○ **2.5ml (½ tsp) cumin**
- ○ **2.5ml (½ tsp) cinnamon**
- ○ **5ml (1 tsp) chopped mint**
- ○ **2 pinches cayenne pepper**
- ○ **15ml (1 tbls) chopped parsley**
- ○ **15ml (1 tbls) chopped coriander**
- ○ **5ml (1 tsp) grated fresh ginger root**
- ○ **juice of ½ lemon**
- ○ **70g (3 oz) butter**
- ○ **salt**

1. Peel and finely chop or grate the onions. Place 15ml (1 tbls) onion in a bowl. Place the remainder in a saucepan, add ½ litre (18 fl oz) water, ginger, butter, salt and 1 pinch cayenne. Bring to the boil, cover and leave to simmer for 30 minutes.
2. Meanwhile prepare the meatballs: add the meat to the bowl containing the onions and add salt, cinnamon, mint, cumin, 1 pinch cayenne, 7.5ml (½ tbls) each parsley and coriander, and work this mixture with your fingers.
3. Shape into balls, no bigger than billiard balls, by rolling them between the palm of your hands. To make this easier and to prevent them from sticking to your fingers, dip your hands in cold water before making each ball.
4. When the onions are tender, pass them, with their sauce, through a mill and return to the pan, then add the meatballs and cook for 7-8 minutes on a low heat. Shake the pan so that the meatballs roll about in the sauce and cook on all sides.
5. When the meatballs are cooked and the onion sauce is creamy and adheres to the meatballs, add the remainder of the coriander and parsley and the lemon juice, mix and remove from the heat. If there is too much sauce, cook a little longer.

Accompany this Moroccan-inspired dish with saffron rice.

Feuilleté aux Groseilles

Serves 6-7. Preparation and cooking: 50 min

Minced Steak in Flaky Pastry with Gooseberries

★

- ○ **500g (18 oz) minced steak**
- ○ **200g (7 oz) onions, finely chopped**
- ○ **100g (4 oz) gooseberries, topped and tailed**
- ○ **30ml (2 tbls) pine nuts**
- ○ **5ml (1 tsp) freshly grated ginger root or powdered ginger**
- ○ **2 pinches mixed spice**
- ○ **5ml (1 tsp) sugar**
- ○ **nutmeg**
- ○ **60g (2¼ oz) butter**
- ○ **600g (21 oz) flaky pastry**
- ○ **30ml (2 tbls) flour**
- ○ **1 egg yolk**
- ○ **salt and pepper**

1. Thaw pastry if frozen. Put the onions in a pan with 50g (2 oz) butter, cook over a low heat for 3-4 minutes, then add the meat and cook over high flame for 2 minutes, mashing with a fork, until all trace of pink has disappeared. Remove from the heat, add sugar, salt, pepper and nutmeg to taste, mixed spice and ginger, stir and allow to cool.
2. Meanwhile, toast the pine nuts in a small pan, without fat, shaking the pan to brown them on all sides, then add to the meat.
3. Cut the pastry in two. Roll out the first half on a lightly floured board, making a square of about 30-35cm (12-14 inches).
4. Grease a baking sheet with the remaining butter. Place the pastry square on it, then spread it with the meat, leaving a 2cm (¾ inch) border. Top with gooseberries.
5. Preheat the oven to 220°C (425°F; gas mark 7). Roll out the remainder of the pastry in a similar square and place it on the gooseberries. Dampen the edges of the first square with a brush dipped in water, press together the edges of both squares with your fingers to seal them, then roll up slightly.
6. Brush the pastry with the beaten egg yolk and bake for 20 to 25 minutes, until well browned.

When fresh gooseberries are out of season, use 15ml (1 tbls) gooseberry jelly and omit the sugar.

Steak Tartare (p64) ▶

Boulettes au Basilic

Serves 4-5. Preparation and cooking: 1 hr

Meatballs with Basil

★

- ○ **400g (14 oz) minced steak**
- ○ **50g (2 oz) white bread, crusts removed**
- ○ **45ml (3 tbls) milk**
- ○ **1 clove garlic**
- ○ **1 egg**
- ○ **45ml (3 tbls) grated Gruyère cheese**
- ○ **30ml (2 tbls) chopped basil**
- ○ **2 medium-sized onions, finely chopped**
- ○ **1kg (2¼ lb) peeled, seeded and crushed tomatoes**
- ○ **30ml (2 tbls) olive oil**
- ○ **salt and pepper**

1. Place the onions in a frying pan with the oil and 200ml (7 fl oz) water. Cover and allow to cook over low heat for 15 minutes, then add the tomatoes and cook uncovered over a medium heat for 20 minutes.
2. Meanwhile, prepare the meatballs. Place the mince in a bowl. Peel the garlic and put through a garlic press into the bowl. Break the egg onto it, add half the basil, salt and pepper to taste, and the cheese, and work this mixture thoroughly with your hands.
3. Heat the milk in small saucepan, crumble in the bread, then remove from the heat and beat with fork until it becomes paste-like, add to the meat and mix.
4. Shape this mixture into balls slightly larger than billiard balls – you should get about 40 – by rolling the mixture in the palms of your hands. To make this easier, dip your hands into cold water between making each ball.
5. When the tomatoes are reduced to one-third of their original quantity (about 20 minutes), add the meatballs and cook for 10 minutes, shaking the pan to cook them on all sides, then remove from the heat. Sprinkle with the remaining basil, place on a hot serving dish and serve immediately.

The ideal accompaniment to these meatballs is noodles, cooked until they are just tender (*al dente*) and lightly buttered. Serve with grated Gruyère or Parmesan cheese.

Fricadelles

Serves 5-6. Preparation: 20 min Cooking: 10 min

Meatballs

★

- ○ **600g (21 oz) minced steak**
- ○ **150g (5 oz) soft butter**
- ○ **100g (4 oz) white bread, crusts removed**
- ○ **90ml (6 tbls) milk**
- ○ **2 eggs**
- ○ **100g (4 oz) onions, finely chopped**
- ○ **100ml (3½ fl oz) oil**
- ○ **nutmeg**
- ○ **salt and pepper**

1. Heat the milk in saucepan, crumble in the bread and work with a fork until a soft, sticky paste is obtained. Put this paste into a bowl and allow to cool.
2. Place the onion in a sauté pan with 20g (¾ oz) butter and sauté on a low heat until transparent (3-4 minutes). Pour the contents of the pan into the bowl, then add the eggs, the mince and the remaining butter, and salt, pepper and nutmeg to taste. Work the mixture with your hands until it is very well blended.
3. Divide into balls the size of an egg – you should obtain a dozen – and flatten them so they are slightly larger than 1cm (½ inch) thick.
4. Heat the oil in a frying pan and brown the meatballs on a low heat for 3-4 minutes each side, then drain on kitchen paper and serve immediately. If you fry them in two lots, keep the first batch warm in a low oven.

Accompany with a vegetable purée.

Feuilles de Chou Farcies

Serves 6. Preparation: 30 min Cooking: 1 hr

Stuffed Cabbage Leaves

★

○ **1 curly white-heart cabbage**
○ **500g (18 oz) minced steak**
○ **250g (9 fl oz) mild-cure bacon**
○ **1 clove garlic**
○ **2 shallots**
○ **15ml (1 tbls) chopped fines herbs: a mixture of parsley, chives, tarragon, chervil**
○ **30ml (2 tbls) oil**
○ **100g (4 oz) grated Gruyère cheese**
○ **250g (9 oz) double cream**
○ **nutmeg**
○ **salt and pepper**

1. Bring a large quantity of water to the boil in a large saucepan. Separate the cabbage leaves carefully. Keep the 12 largest, wash them and when the water boils, add salt and plunge the leaves in the water for 1 minute to soften them. Remove and plunge into a bowl of cold water, drain and spread out on a cloth. Wash the rest of the cabbage and blanch for 5 minutes, then drain in a sieve, pressing all the water out. Chop finely, having first removed the veins of the largest leaves.
2. Chop the bacon as finely as possible. Peel the shallots and chop finely. Peel the garlic. Heat 15ml (1 tbls) oil in a large pan, add the bacon and shallots and lightly brown for 3 minutes over a low heat. Add the minced steak and cook for 5 minutes, stirring with a fork. Add the chopped cabbage, stir and cook for a further 2 minutes, then turn off the heat. Add salt, pepper and nutmeg to taste, and the herbs. Put the garlic through a garlic press into the pan. Mix again and allow to cool.
3. Preheat the oven to 200°C (400°F; gas mark 6). Divide the stuffing between the 12 cabbage leaves. Fold each over as if making a small parcel. With the remaining oil, grease an ovenproof dish large enough to hold the cabbage leaves in one layer, arrange the small parcels closely, then add enough water to almost cover them.
4. Bake for 1 hour. After 45 minutes, sprinkle with grated cheese and, 5 minutes before they are done, pour over the cream.

Serve very hot, accompanied by mashed potatoes.

Steak aux Trois Fromages et au Persil

Serves 4. Preparation: 10 min Cooking: 8 min

Minced Steak with Cheese and Parsley

★

○ **600g (21 oz) minced steak**
○ **60ml (4 tbls) curd cheese**
○ **60ml (4 tbls) grated Gruyère cheese**
○ **60ml (4 tbls) grated Parmesan cheese**
○ **30ml (2 tbls) chopped parsley**
○ **45ml (3 tbls) oil**
○ **nutmeg**
○ **salt and pepper**

1. Put the undrained curd cheese in a bowl and beat it until it is smooth. Add the mince and work the mixture until it is very well blended, then add the Parmesan, Gruyère, parsley, and salt, pepper and nutmeg to taste. Work again with your hands until everything is well blended.
2. Divide the mixture into 4 equal parts, then flatten each one and shape into an oval or round, 1.5cm (slightly more than ½ inch) thick.
3. Heat the oil in a sauté pan and lightly brown the steaks for about 4 minutes on each side, over a low heat. When the steaks are browned, remove from the pan with a skimmer and serve immediately.

Cassolettes au Maïs

Tamale Pies

Serves 4. Preparation and cooking: 2 hr

★★

○ **600g (21 oz) minced steak**
○ **600g (21 oz) ripe tomatoes**
○ **2 large onions**
○ **2 red peppers**
○ **2 cloves garlic**
○ **15ml (1 tbls) tomato purée**
○ **15ml (1 tbls) paprika**
○ **2.5ml (½ tsp) cayenne pepper**
○ **2.5ml (½ tsp) cinnamon**
○ **2 cloves**
○ **10ml (2 tsp) sugar**
○ **350g (12 oz) maize flour (polenta)**
○ **80g (3½ oz) butter**
○ **45ml (3 tbls) olive oil**
○ **salt**

1. Boil some water in a saucepan, immerse the tomatoes for 10 seconds, then peel, cut into halves, remove their seeds and mash roughly with a fork.
2. Peel and finely chop the onions. Wash the peppers, cut into quarters and remove the seeds and white filaments. Cut into 5mm (¼ inch) squares.
3. Heat 30ml (2 tbls) oil in a sauté pan and the remaining 15ml (1 tbls) in a small pan. Put the onions into the sauté pan and the peppers into the small pan and cook both over a low heat, without allowing them to brown, for about 10 minutes.
4. At the end of this time add the mince to the sauté pan and cook, mashing it with a spatula, over a high flame for 5 minutes or until browned, then add the sautéed peppers, tomatoes, paprika, cayenne, cinnamon, cloves and salt. Peel the garlic and put through a garlic press into the sauté pan. Mix. Dilute the tomato purée in ½ litre (18 fl oz) water and add to the pan with 5ml (1 tsp) sugar. Mix, cover and allow to simmer for 1 hour, stirring now and then.
5. 15 minutes before the end of cooking time, preheat the oven to 200°C (400°F; gas mark 6). Pour 1 litre (1¾ pints) water into a large saucepan, add the remaining sugar, a little salt and 50g (2 oz) butter. When the water boils, quickly add the maize flour, stirring. Cook for 3 minutes and remove from the heat. This mixture should not be completely cooked and must still be soft.
6. With the remaining butter, grease the insides of 4 soufflé dishes or small casseroles of ½ litre (18 fl oz) capacity. Coat the bottom and sides with a layer 1cm (½ inch) thick of maize flour paste using the back of a spoon. When the meat is cooked – there should be very little sauce remaining – divide the contents of the sauté pan among the 4 dishes, cover each with aluminium foil or with their own lids if they have them, and bake for 30 minutes.
7. Remove the foil or lids, place the dishes on plates and serve.

These pies were inspired by the Mexican *tamales*, which are wrapped in maize husks and steamed.

Hamburger Steak

Hamburgers

Serves 4. Preparation and cooking: 20 min

★

○ **800g (1¾ lb) minced steak**
○ **4 medium-sized onions, finely chopped**
○ **60g (2½ oz) butter**
○ **15ml (1 tbls) oil**
○ **salt and pepper**

1. Melt 40g (1¾ oz) of butter in a frying pan, add the onions. Sweat over a very low heat until they are transparent; they must not be browned.
2. Put the meat in a bowl, sprinkle with the salt and pepper, and add to it the contents of the frying pan. Mix. Divide the mixture into 4. Roll into balls and flatten them until 1.5cm (½ inch) thick.
3. Put the rest of the butter and oil in the frying pan used to cook the onions. Remove all the pieces of onions which are still in it, because they will burn and give a pungent taste to the meat. Fry the steaks for 5 to 7 minutes until they are well brown.

Russian Hamburgers (p64) ▶

Palets du Poitou à la Moelle

Serves 6. Preparation: 20 min Cooking: 15 min

Beef Marrow Rissoles

★

- ○ **600g (21 oz) minced steak**
- ○ **300g (10 oz) beef marrow**
- ○ **100g (4 oz) white bread, crusts removed**
- ○ **150ml (5 fl oz) milk**
- ○ **2 eggs**
- ○ **2 medium-sized onions, finely chopped**
- ○ **45ml (3 tbls) oil**
- ○ **50g (2 oz) butter**
- ○ **30ml (2 tbls) white wine**
- ○ **juice of 1 lemon**
- ○ **15ml (1 tbls) chopped parsley**
- ○ **nutmeg**
- ○ **salt and pepper**

1. Heat the milk in a saucepan, add the crumbled bread, stirring with a spatula until a smooth and sticky paste is obtained, then remove from the heat and allow to cool.
2. Place onions in a pan with 25g (1 oz) butter over a low heat. Cook, stirring occasionally, until slightly browned, then remove from the heat.
3. Mash the marrow in a bowl with a fork, add the mince, mix and add the bread and browned onions. Break in the eggs, add salt, pepper and nutmeg to taste and work the mixture with one hand until well blended.
4. Divide the mixture into 8 equal parts, roll into balls, then flatten into rissoles 1.5cm (slightly more than ½ inch) thick. Moisten your hands with water to prevent the mixture from sticking to your fingers.
5. Heat the oil in a frying pan, add the remaining butter and, when melted, brown the rissoles for 15 minutes over a low heat, turning once. When cooked, place on a serving dish and keep warm (they must be eaten very hot) in a low oven.
6. Discard the cooking fat, deglaze the pan with the white wine, scraping up the crusty bits on the bottom, allow the wine to evaporate then add the lemon juice and parsley. Pour over the rissoles and serve immediately.

Croquettes aux Champignons

Serves 4. Preparation: 30 min Cooking: 20 min

Meatballs with Dried Mushrooms

★ ★

- ○ **40g (1¾ oz) dried mushrooms**
- ○ **400g (14 oz) minced flank**
- ○ **100g (4 oz) mortadella sausage**
- ○ **100g (4 oz) Emmenthal cheese, grated**
- ○ **small bunch basil**
- ○ **2 eggs**
- ○ **salt and pepper**
- ○ **1 pinch grated nutmeg**
- ○ **flour**
- ○ **½ onion**
- ○ **40g (1¾ oz) butter**
- ○ **45ml (3 tbls) oil**
- ○ **30ml (2 tbls) tomato purée**

1. Soak the dried mushrooms in tepid water for ½ hour. Then wash them thoroughly and chop very finely.
2. Meanwhile, place the meat in a bowl and add the mortadella (put twice through a mincer), mushrooms, grated cheese, chopped basil, eggs, a pinch each of salt, pepper and grated nutmeg. Mix with a wooden spoon until well blended, then divide into balls the size of an apricot. Coat these in flour.
3. Brown the chopped onion in the butter and hot oil in a large pan. Add the meatballs, brown them on all sides, then add 150ml (5 fl oz) water mixed with the tomato purée. Add salt and pepper and cook for about 20 minutes over a low heat, turning often. Then turn into a hot serving dish and serve immediately.

Croquette Géante aux Oeufs Durs

Meatloaf with Hard-boiled Eggs

Serves 6. Preparation: 30 min
Cooking 1 hr 15 min
★★

○ **1kg (2¼ lb) minced steak**
○ **5 eggs**
○ **1kg (2¼ lb) peeled, seeded and crushed tomatoes**
○ **2 medium-sized onions**
○ **2 cloves garlic**
○ **2.5ml (½ tsp) cumin powder**
○ **2 pinches cayenne pepper**
○ **nutmeg**
○ **15ml (1 tbls) flour**
○ **30ml (2 tbls) dry breadcrumbs**
○ **60ml (4 tbls) oil**
○ **salt and pepper**

1. Peel the onions and chop finely. Heat 30ml (2 tbls) oil in a saucepan. Cook the onions for 2 minutes, without allowing them to brown. Then add the tomatoes and simmer over a low heat for 15 minutes.
2. Boil some water in a saucepan and cook 4 eggs for 8 minutes, then run cold water over them.
3. While the eggs are cooking, place the meat in a bowl, add salt, pepper and nutmeg to taste, cumin and cayenne. Peel the garlic and put through a garlic press into the bowl. Break in the remaining egg. Mix everything together, using your hands. When the boiled eggs are cold, shell them and trim both ends so that the yolk shows.
4. Dust a working surface with flour and spread the meat into a square the length of the eggs put end to end. Place the eggs in a row down the centre and roll up. Round off the ends and dust the roll with the breadcrumbs.
5. Heat the remaining oil in a frying pan and lightly brown the roll for 8-10 minutes on all sides.
6. When the tomatoes have cooked for 15 minutes, add them to the frying pan. Add salt and pepper to taste, cover and simmer for 45 minutes over a low heat, turning from time to time.
7. Slice the meatloaf and serve, with the sauce in a sauceboat.

Accompany with rice, fried aubergines or sautéed courgettes. This meatloaf can be cooked in wine, beef stock or water instead of the tomato sauce.

Roulade aux Légumes

Vegetable Roll

Serves 6. Preparation: 30 min Cooking: 2 hr
Refrigeration: overnight
★★

○ **1kg (2¼ lb) flank or brisket**
○ **200g (7 oz) fresh spinach**
○ **6 medium-sized carrots**
○ **2 medium-sized onions**
○ **2 cloves garlic**
○ **60ml (4 tbls) chopped parsley**
○ **5ml (1 tsp) thyme leaves**
○ **4 hard-boiled eggs**
○ **salt and pepper**

1. Ask your butcher to flatten, as much as possible, a slice of flank or brisket, having made a horizontal cut along the grain without cutting the meat through.
2. Remove the spinach stalks, wash and drain the leaves. Peel the onions and slice into thin rounds. Peel the carrots and cut in two down the middle. Peel the garlic, and chop finely and mix with the parsley. Shell the hard-boiled eggs and slice into rounds.
3. Spread the meat on a working surface, add salt, pepper and thyme, cover the meat with spinach and spread the garlic-parsley mixture over the spinach. You will be rolling up the meat along the width of the rectangle: keeping this in mind, arrange alternate rows of carrots and eggs. Cover with onion rings; add more salt and pepper.
4. Preheat the oven to 200°C (400°F; gas mark 6). Roll up the meat and vegetables. Bind with string like a roast.
5. Place the roll in an oval dish just large enough to hold it. Add cold water to barely cover the meat, and salt to taste. Cover and bake for 2 hours.
6. When the roll is cooked, remove from the dish, allow to drain, then roll in a piece of aluminium foil and leave to cool before refrigerating.
7. Serve the vegetable roll cold the following day, cut into thin slices, as an hors d'oeuvre or the main dish of a summer meal.

Accompany this dish (of Argentinian origin) with a green salad and pickled gherkins.

Terrine aux Poireaux et à la Menthe

Minced Beef with Leeks and Mint

Serves 5-6. Preparation: 25 min
Cooking: 2 hr Refrigeration: 8 hr
★★

○ **500g (18 oz) minced chuck or silverside**
○ **1kg (2¼ lb) leeks**
○ **50g (2 oz) bread, crusts removed**
○ **100ml (3½ fl oz) double cream**
○ **1 egg**
○ **15ml (1 tbls) chopped mint**
○ **100g (4 oz) shelled peas (petits pois if available)**
○ **nutmeg**
○ **15ml (1 tbls) oil**
○ **salt and pepper**

1. Peel the leeks, cut part of the green away, weigh and keep 500g (18 oz). Cut into rounds 3mm (⅛ inch) long. Bring some water to the boil in a large pan, add salt and blanch the leeks for 3 minutes, then drain in a sieve, pressing to extract all the water.
2. Heat the cream in a small saucepan, crumble in the bread and mix to obtain a sticky paste, then remove from the heat.
3. Place the meat in a bowl, sprinkle generously with nutmeg, salt and pepper, add the bread paste and knead with your hands until well blended. Add the leeks, mix again, then the egg and mint, and work until you have a compact mixture.
4. Preheat the oven to 140°C (275°F; gas mark 1). Lightly oil an ovenproof dish. Place in it a layer of one-third of the beef mixture, press down well, scatter peas here and there, then put in another third of the mixture, then the rest of the peas and finish with a layer of meat. Press down well and brush the top with oil. Cover and bake for 2 hours.
5. At the end of this time, remove from the oven and allow to cool at least 8 hours before serving.

Accompany with a sweet-and-sour tomato sauce.

Rillettes de Queue de Boeuf

Potted Oxtail

Serves 6. Preparation: 20 min Cooking: 4-5 hr
Refrigeration: 8 hr
★★

○ **1.5kg (3¼ lb) oxtail (the fleshy part)**
○ **750ml (1 bottle) red wine: Beaujolais or Côtes du Rhône**
○ **2 large ripe tomatoes**
○ **200g (7 oz) carrots**
○ **250g (9 oz) onions**
○ **6 shallots**
○ **2 cloves garlic**
○ **100g (4 oz) button mushrooms**
○ **juice of ½ lemon**
○ **3 cloves**
○ **6 sprigs parsley**
○ **1 stick celery**
○ **1 bay leaf**
○ **1 sprig thyme**
○ **1 slice orange peel, 2cm (¾ inch) by 3cm (1¼ inches)**
○ **15ml (1 tbls) chopped fines herbes: a mixture of parsley, chives, tarragon, chervil**
○ **45ml (3 tbls) oil**
○ **salt and pepper**

1. Cut the oxtail into pieces 4cm (1½ inches) long. Cut the tomatoes in half, press to remove the seeds and crush. Peel the carrots and cut into rounds. Leave 1 onion whole and spike it with cloves. Peel and roughly chop the shallots and the remainder of the onions. Trim the earthy base off the mushrooms. Wash, wipe dry, cut into quarters and sprinkle with lemon juice. Wrap the orange peel, thyme and bay leaf in the celery and parsley and bind with thread to form a bouquet garni.
2. Heat the oil in a pan and lightly brown the pieces of oxtail, removing them when they are done, and put aside. Add to the pan the carrot rounds, shallots and chopped onions and allow to brown lightly, then add the oxtail, bouquet garni, peeled garlic, tomatoes, mushrooms and their juice, and barely cover with wine. Add salt. Bring to the boil, cover the pan and allow to simmer for 4-5 hours, until the flesh is tender and comes away from the bone easily.
3. Remove the pieces of oxtail, sieve the juice, put the vegetables aside and reduce the juice until only about 240ml (9 fl oz) remains. Remove from the heat.
4. Remove the meat from the bones and shred with a fork. Put the vegetables – except the onion spiked with cloves and the bouquet garni – through a vegetable mill. Skim the fat from the gravy, add vegetable purée, meat and *fines herbes*. Add pepper to taste, mix and place in an earthenware dish. Leave to cool for 8 hours before serving.

Accompany with a green or mixed salad, gherkins, small pickled onions and toast.

Swiss Salad (p78) ▶

Daube de Joue en Gelée
Jellied Beef Cheek

Serves 6. Preparation: 20 min Cooking: 2½-3 hr
Refrigeration: 8 hr
★ ★

○ **1kg (2¼ lb) cheek of beef**
○ **2 calf's feet**
○ **24 small onions**
○ **3 carrots**
○ **1 clove garlic**
○ **1 sprig thyme**
○ **1 bay leaf**
○ **6 sprigs parsley**
○ **1 piece orange peel, 2cm**
  (¾ inch) by 3cm (1¼ inches)
○ **15ml (1 tbls) cognac**
○ **½ litre (18 fl oz) white wine**
○ **5ml (1 tsp) peppercorns**
○ **salt**

1. Halve the calf's feet and blanch in boiling water for 10 minutes. Peel the carrots and cut into cubes 1cm (½ inch) square. Peel the onions. Peel and crush the garlic and wrap in the parsley sprigs, together with the orange peel, thyme and bay leaf. Tie together with white thread to make a bouquet garni.
2. In a stewpan, place the calf's feet, pieces of cheek, carrots, onions, bouquet garni, salt, pepper and cognac, and moisten with white wine, which should just cover the stew. If it does not, add water. Cover and bring to the boil. Simmer for 2½ to 3 hours, until the meat is very tender.
3. Remove the calf's feet from the pan, take out the bones, cut the flesh into small cubes and return to the pan. Discard the bouquet garni. Leave to cool, then pour everything into a terrine, mixing so that the contents are distributed equally. Put in a cold place for at least 8 hours. Dip the dish in hot water for 3 minutes then turn out.

Serve with a salad and garlic bread.

Terrine de Foie
Calf's Liver Terrine

Serves 6. Preparation: 30 min Cooking: 1 hr 30 min
Refrigeration: 12 hr
★ ★

○ **500g (18 oz) calf's liver**
○ **200g (7 oz) mild-cure bacon**
○ **200g (7 oz) sausagemeat**
○ **250g (9 oz) sliced bacon**
○ **50ml (1¾ fl oz) cognac**
○ **50ml (1¾ fl oz) Madeira**
○ **2 pinches mixed spice**
○ **1 clove garlic**
○ **3 sprigs thyme**
○ **3 bay leaves**
○ **2.5ml (½ tsp) thyme leaves**
○ **30ml (2 tbls) chopped parsley**
○ **salt and pepper**

1. Cut the liver into cubes 1cm (½ inch) square. Place in a bowl, add salt and pepper, mixed spice and thyme leaves and mix.
2. Chop the mild-cure bacon into small pieces. Peel the garlic and put through a garlic press into the bowl.
3. Add the sausagemeat and chopped bacon to the bowl. Mix well, then moisten with cognac and Madeira and mix again.
4. Cover the bottom and sides of a terrine just big enough to contain the mixture with slices of bacon. Preheat the oven to 230°C (450°F; gas mark 8).
5. Pour the contents of the bowl into the terrine. Thinly slice the rest of the bacon and criss-cross the slices over the meat mixture. Decorate with thyme sprigs and bay leaves. Cover. Place the terrine in a larger pan containing hot water and cook for ½ hour at 230°C, then lower the heat to 200°C (400°F; gas mark 6) and cook for 1 hour.
6. When the terrine is cooked, remove from the oven, leave to cool completely, then refrigerate for 12 hours before serving.

Serve with pickled gherkins and small pickled onions.

Pâtés always shrink a little during cooking. It is very useful to have in your kitchen the same type of dish in several sizes so a pâté cooked in one dish can be served in another, slightly smaller one.

Boeuf à l'Anis Étoilé

Beef with Star Anise

Serves 6-7. Preparation: 20 min Cooking: 3½-4 hr
Refrigeration: overnight
★★

○ **1kg (2¼ lb) rump or silverside, bound**
○ **1 calf's foot, cut in two**
○ **200ml (7 fl oz) rice wine, white wine or dry sherry**
○ **100ml (3½ fl oz) soya sauce**
○ **1 piece ginger root, 2cm by 3cm (¾ inch by 1¼ inches)**
○ **4 heads star anise**
○ **15ml (1 tbls) sugar**

1. Boil some water in a large saucepan, then add the beef and calf's foot and simmer for 10 minutes. Discard the water. Place the beef in a stewpan just big enough to hold it, rinse the calf's foot in cold water and add to the stewpan. Peel the ginger root, slice thinly and add, along with the anise, soya sauce, wine and sugar. Add water to barely cover the meat.
2. Place over a low heat, bring to the boil, then simmer for 3½ to 4 hours, partially covered, until the meat is tender and can easily be pierced by a knife.
3. Leave the beef to cool in the sauce for 2 hours, then remove from the sauce, wrap in aluminium foil and put in the refrigerator. Discard the calf's foot, skim the fat from the sauce and pass it through a sieve. Reduce over a high flame until about 240ml (9 fl oz) remains. Pour this into a small mould and refrigerate overnight.
4. The next day, slice the meat as thinly as possible and arrange on a serving dish. Plunge the mould containing the jelly into hot water for 10 seconds, then unmould, cut the jelly into small cubes and decorate the meat.

Accompany with a green salad, vegetables in sweet-and-sour sauce or pickled onions. This Chinese-style beef can also be served hot. In this case add 15ml (1 tbls) sesame oil to the sauce after it is reduced and pour over the sliced beef.

Terrine au Persil

Parsley Terrine

Serves 6. Preparation: 45 min Cooking: 2 hr 30 min
Refrigeration: 4 hr
★★

○ **750g (1 lb 10 oz) blade**
○ **250g (9 oz) mild-cure bacon**
○ **300g (10 oz) cooked ham**
○ **1 very large bunch parsley**
○ **2 cloves garlic**
○ **100g (4 oz) dry breadcrumbs**
○ **45ml (3 tbls) armagnac**
○ **45ml (3 tbls) sherry**
○ **3 bay leaves**
○ **3 sprigs thyme**
○ **15ml (1 tbls) oil**
○ **salt and pepper**

1. Cut the beef into very thin slices, then into strips 1cm (½ inch) by 2cm (¾ inch) and place in a bowl. Salt and pepper lightly, sprinkle with sherry and armagnac and mix.
2. Remove the rind from the bacon and cut into very thin strips. Chop the ham and mix with the bacon.
3. Wash and dry the parsley. Chop the leaves and the softest part of the stalks, not too small. Peel the garlic, chop finely and mix with the parsley.
4. Preheat the oven to 170°C (325°F; gas mark 3). Oil a terrine which is just large enough to hold all the ingredients. Cover the bottom with one-third of the beef, then half the bacon-ham mixture, then a layer of parsley, then 30ml (2 tbls) breadcrumbs. Continue in the same way until all the ingredients are used up. Pour the beef marinade into the dish before finishing with a layer of breadcrumbs. Press down well, place the bay leaves and thyme sprigs on top and cover.
5. Bake for 2½ hours, then remove from the oven and cool completely before serving with a salad, pickled gherkins or small pickled onions.

Saucisson aux Piments à l'Antillaise

Sausage with Hot Peppers

Serves 6. Preparation: 20 min
Cooking: 1 hr 30 min Refrigeration: 4 hr
★★

○ **500g (18 oz) minced silverside or chuck**
○ **250g (9 oz) prawns, peeled and chopped**
○ **200g (7 oz) ham, chopped**
○ **1 medium-sized onion**
○ **2 cloves garlic**
○ **2 fresh hot red peppers**
○ **200g (7 oz) shelled peas (petit pois if available)**
○ **90ml (6 tbls) dry breadcrumbs**
○ **2 eggs**
○ **2 bay leaves**
○ **salt**

1. In a bowl, mix the mince, ham and prawns. Peel the garlic and put through a garlic press into the bowl. Peel and grate the onions, chop the peppers and add to the bowl with 30ml (2 tbls) breadcrumbs. Add salt. Break 1 egg into the bowl and work the mixture with your hands until it is well blended and compact, then add the peas and mix carefully.
2. Form the mixture into a sausage 25cm (10 inches) long, moistening your hands with water to make it easier.
3. Beat the second egg in a bowl and brush the sausage with it, then roll in the remaining breadcrumbs. Wrap the sausage tightly in muslin and tie the two ends.
4. Boil some water in a large oval pan, add salt and the bay leaf, and plunge in the sausage, which must be completely immersed. Simmer for 1½ hours.
5. At the end of this time, remove the sausage from the pan and let it cool completely before removing the muslin.

Serve thinly sliced with salads and a cold sweet-and-sour tomato sauce. You can substitute unsweetened cracker or biscuit crumbs for the breadcrumbs.

Salade Suisse

Swiss Salad

Serves 4. Preparation and cooking: 45 min
★

○ **600g (21 oz) potatoes**
○ **1 cucumber, thinly sliced**
○ **300g (10 oz) fillet**
○ **45ml (3 tbls) mustard**
○ **75ml (2½ fl oz) milk**
○ **2 raw egg yolks**
○ **1 hard-boiled egg**
○ **small handful capers**
○ **salt and pepper**

1. Boil the potatoes, peel and slice while they are still warm. Arrange a layer of potatoes decoratively in a bowl, top with the cucumber slices in a ring, and then with the fillet, cut into small pieces.
2. Blend the mustard with the milk, beating until completely amalgamated, then add the raw egg yolks and crumbled hard-boiled egg.
3. Pour this sauce over the meat and vegetables, sprinkle with capers and add salt and pepper. Mix together at the table.

When you are cooking a dish to serve cold, or are preparing something in advance which you will be reheating later, cool it quickly at room temperature, then refrigerate it. (Refrigerating hot food is not a good idea – it will eventually damage your refrigerator.)

Meatballs with Dried Mushrooms (p72) ➤

Wines: the Finishing Touch

Nowadays excellent quality table wines are within the reach of everyone, though you should expect to pay more for a good vintage wine from one of the famous vineyards, such as Nuits-St-Georges or Schloss Johannisberg Riesling. When buying French wine, look for the *Appellation Contrôlée* label, which is a guarantee of quality.

Below is a guide to the wines that go best with certain foods, but there are no absolute *rules* about which wine to serve with what food – in the end it is your palate that must decide. For a large, formal meal, certain wines traditionally follow each other through the menu and you could serve three or even four wines at one meal. In this case, it is usual to serve dry sherry with the soup, dry white wine with the fish course, claret or burgundy with the meat or game and a white dessert wine or medium sweet champagne with the dessert. For cheese, your guests would return to the claret or burgundy. Certain foods kill the flavour of wine and should therefore be avoided if you are planning to serve wine with the meal. Mint sauce, for example, or any salad with a strong vinaigrette dressing, will destroy the taste of the wine.

Remember that red wines are generally served *chambré*, or at room temperature, to bring out the flavour. Draw the cork at least three or four hours before you plan to drink the wine and let the bottle stand in the kitchen or a warm room. (Never be tempted into putting the bottle in hot water or in front of the fire – the flavour will be ruined.) The exception to the *chambré* rule is Beaujolais, which can be served cool – some people even serve it chilled. White or rosé wines are usually served chilled – the easiest way is to put them in the fridge an hour before serving, or plunge them into an ice bucket, if you have one. Champagne should also be served well chilled and is generally brought to the table in an ice bucket.

Wines to Serve with Food

Oysters, shellfish	Chablis, dry Moselle, Champagne
Fried or grilled fish	Dry Graves, Moselle, Hock, Rosé, Blanc de Blanc
Fish with sauces	Riesling, Pouilly-Fuissé, Chablis
Veal, pork or chicken dishes (served simply)	Rosé, Riesling, a light red wine such as Beaujolais
Chicken or pork served with a rich sauce	Claret, Côte de Rhône, Médoc
Rich meat dishes, steaks, game	Red Burgundy, Rioja, Red Chianti
Lamb or duck	Claret, Beaujolais
Desserts and puddings	White Bordeaux, Sauternes, Entre Deux Mers
Cheese	Burgundy, Rioja, Cabernet Sauvignon

This edition published 1981 by Ferndale Editions, Brent House, 24-28 Friern Park, London N12, England under licence from the proprietor, Curcio Periodici, Rome

Translated from the French edition published by Hachette, Paris
Designed by Selina Graphics, London

© 1976 by Curcio Periodici, Rome
© 1981 English translation, Brigitte PMF Fauny

ISBN 0 905746 32 5

Printed and bound in Hong Kong by South China Printing Company